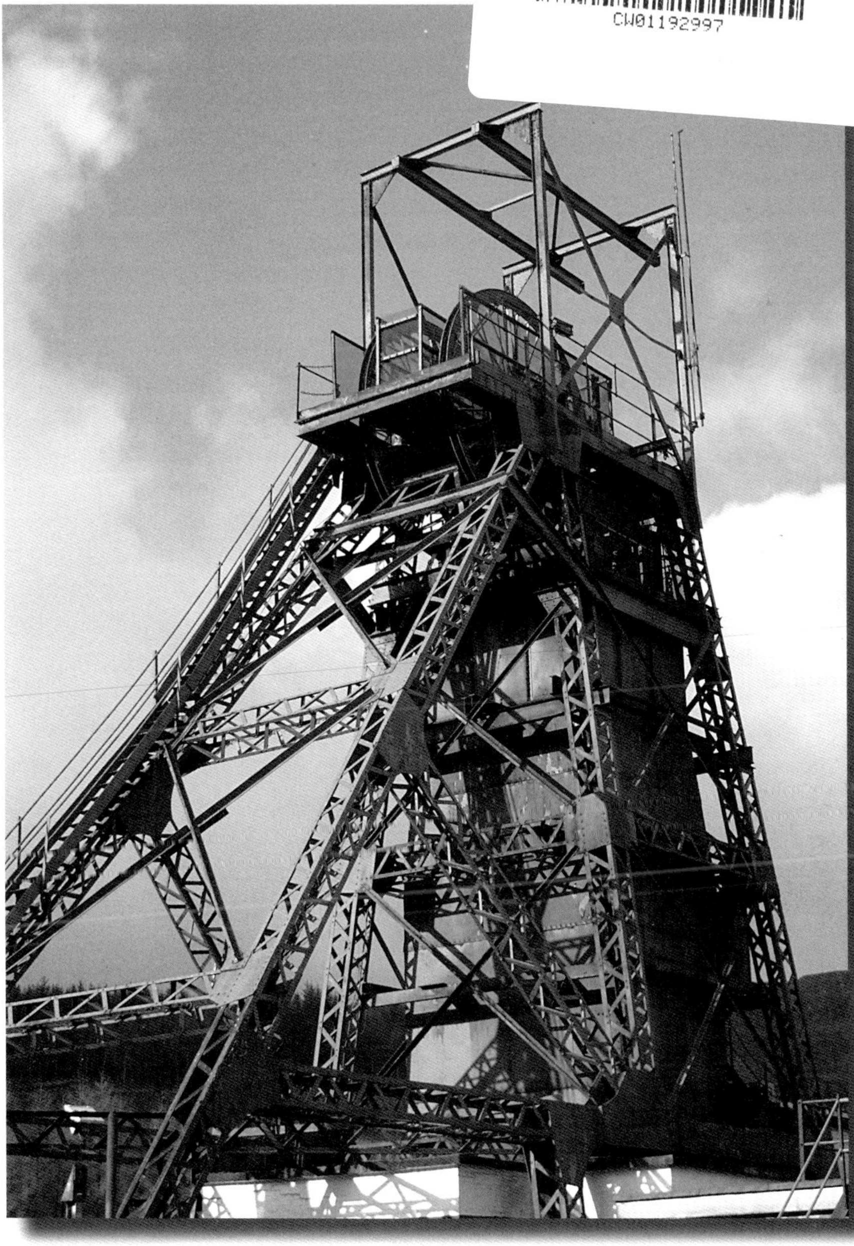

1984 – THE GREAT COAL STRIKE

By Hedley McCarthy

May 2009

'Then there comes a man with a paper and a pen
Tellin' us our hard times are about to end.
And then, if they don't give us what we like
He said, "Men, that's when you gotta go on strike."

King Harvest (Has Surely Come,) Robbie Robertson, 1969.

Published by Hedley McCarthy, May 2009.
Copyright © 2009 Hedley McCarthy.

ISBN 978-0-9562543-0-6

Designed and Printed by Steve Thomas.

A quarter of a century ago, in the "Orwellian" year of 1984 the National Union of Mineworkers embarked on their colossal struggle. I instinctively knew at the time that we were about to witness momentous events. I decided I would attempt to record these events as they unfolded week by week.

As a steelworker, living in the heart of the South Wales coalfield and as a Labour councillor in Neil Kinnock's Islwyn constituency I realised I had a good vantage point. Apart from all the press and media coverage I was able to either personally witness or receive at first hand many of the major happenings and each was then written down and filed away. I know that I have not recorded everything, not every act of bravery, comradeship or deceit. Not all of the 11,291 arrests are documented and I have left the machinations of Special Branch and MI5 to others.

If I have not adequately portrayed the hardship and privation suffered then I apologise to all the men and women who struggled in a noble cause and in doing so created history.

Hedley McCarthy April 2009.

Hedley McCarthy is a former Islwyn Borough Councillor who was arrested on a NUM picket line at Port Talbot in July 1984. A former senior Trade Union official at BSC Ebbw Vale, he is a current Blaenau Gwent Councillor (Labour, Llanhilleth ward) and was briefly leader of the Council.

He has an Honours Degree in Social and Labour Studies from the University of Wales Newport.

Foreword By The Rt Hon Paul Murphy M.P. Secretary Of State For Wales

It is with great delight that I recommend to you Hedley McCarthy's history of the 1984/5 Miners' Strike.

I come from a family of colliers – my grandfather and my father went "down the pit" when they were fourteen years of age. As a boy, living in the Eastern Valley of Monmouthshire, my life, like Hedley's was deeply affected by the coal industry and we were aware of the great courage of the South Wales miners.

Hedley's fascinating and readable book tells the moving story of the strike which affected hundreds of people all over the country just a quarter of a century ago. I was a councillor in Torfaen at the time, and the whole community stood firmly behind the miners and their titanic struggle to keep the pits open. Even though Mrs Thatcher's Government got its way, the mining communities saw their men return to work with pride and with dignity.

Hedley lived through all of this and kept a detailed account, week by week. He writes of the personal tragedies, the politics, the personalities, the bravery and fortitude of the miners themselves, and of the women who played such a major part in that year. He has done us all a great service by reminding us about what took place twenty-five years ago. He writes from the heart, but also with the experience of being an active politician in the Gwent Valleys. The book is truly a "labour of love" and no-one can but be moved by his remarkable skill in recounting the difficult and, in some ways, tragic months.

I hope you enjoy this book as much as I did.

Rt Hon Paul Murphy MP
Secretary of State for Wales

1984 - The Great Coal Strike, Table Of Contents.

Setting The Scene *8*
Week 1 - "Here We Go" *14*
Week 2 - A Paramilitary State *17*
Week 3 - Coal vs Steel *19*
Week 4 - Flashpoint - Port Talbot *21*
Week 5 - Flashpoint - Sheffield *23*
Week 6 - The Rule Change *25*
Week 7 - Hardship Funds *28*
Week 8 - The Triple Alliance *30*
Week 9 - Flashpoint - Ravenscraig *32*
Week 10 - Flashpoint - Mansfield *33*
Week 11 - Conciliatory Tone *35*
Week 12 - Flashpoint - Orgreave *37*
Week 13 - Flashpoint - Westminster *40*
Week 14 - Other Forces At Work *43*
Week 15 - "Unlawful Assembly" *46*
Week 16 - The Convoy *48*
Week 17 - "Constructive Discussions" *50*
Week 18 - The First Dock Strike *52*
Week 19 - The End Of The First Dock Strike *54*
Week 20 - The Silver Birch *57*
Week 21 - Seizure Of South Wales Assets *58*
Week 22 - Flashpoint - Harworth *60*
Week 23 - The Spirit Of '39 .... *61*
Week 24 - Flashpoint - Armthorpe/The Second Dock Strike *63*
Week 25 - "Industrial Crisis" *65*
Week 26 - Brighton - Trades Union Congress *67*
Week 27 - End Of The Second Dock Strike - Imminent *70*
Week 28 - Divine Intervention *73*
Week 29 - Flashpoint - Maltby *75*
Week 30 - Blackpool - Labour Party Conference *77*
Week 31 - Brighton - Conservative Party Conference *80*
Week 32 - Flashpoint - Grimethorpe *82*
Week 33 - Sequestration *83*
Week 34 - The Libyan Affair *85*
Week 35 - The Christmas Bonus *88*
Week 36 - No Noose Is Good News *90*
Week 37 - "A Gratuitously Vindictive Act" *92*

Week 38 - The Price Of Coal *94*
Week 39 - The Receiver *96*
Week 40 - Walker Meets The TUC *98*
Week 41 - The Spectre Of Spencerism *100*
Weeks 42 and 43 - Christmas '84 New Year '85 .... *101*
Week 44 - The National Executive *105*
Week 45 - "General Secretary In Exile" *107*
Week 46 - "Impossible Demands" *109*
Week 47 - An Exchange Of Letters *112*
Week 48 - The Joint Statement *114*
Week 49 - Willis Meets MacGregor *116*
Week 50 - Negotiations By Proxy *117*
Week 51 - An Organised Return To Work? *120*
Week 52 - The Strike Ends And The Immediate Aftermath. *122*
Aftermath - The Legacy Of Bitterness *124*

Setting The Scene

Before the protracted, often complicated and always bitter story of the 1984 - 85 miners' strike unfolds it is essential to examine the equally complicated background of events which eventually ignited the dispute.

Firstly it is worth remembering that when Arthur Scargill, (then president of the Yorkshire NUM) was elected to succeed Joe Gormley as president of the National Union of Mineworkers, he was elected with a record majority and yet despite this enormous popularity at the time of his election in 1981, he had since failed to carry the Union membership with him in national ballots for strike action on three separate occasions. Arthur Scargill was President-elect in January 1982 and president at the time of the two other rejections in October 1982 and March 1983. The ballots for strike action had been called by the National Executive of the NUM on both pit closures and wage improvements. The third defeat for the Executive was against the recommendation to take industrial action in protest at the closure of Ty-Mawr-Lewis Merthyr Colliery in South Wales. Scargill had consistently claimed that the National Coal Board had a hit-list of mines proposed for closure, which was denied with equal consistency by the NCB.

Secondly the appointment of Ian MacGregor to replace Norman Siddall as Chairman of The National Coal Board was seen in many quarters of the trade union and Labour movement as a political appointment by The Conservative Government. Confrontation was widely forecast as it was anticipated that MacGregor would undertake a large de-manning exercise in the coal industry. There was a blue print for such speculation as Ian MacGregor had been chairman of The British Steel Corporation when The BSC carried out its massive de-manning operation. This many people believed, was made possible as a result of the thirteen and a half week steel-strike in 1980. Because the strike appeared to have been deliberately triggered by the BSC, offering the steel-unions a derisory 2% pay rise, the dispute highlighted the weakness of those unions and took away the resistance to the huge job losses subsequently suffered in that industry. MacGregor's appointment as BSC Chairman had sparked a major row in Parliament at the time of its announcement. MacGregor the Scottish born American captain of industry (coal and steel) was a known monetarist, therefore practicing the brand of economics much favoured by Mrs Margaret Thatcher's Conservative Government.

The government had paid one and a half million pounds to secure his services as Chairman of BSC, he had built for himself a formidable reputation as a hard liner in American industrial relations, coupled with a spell as Deputy Chairman at British Leyland. So from the time of his appointment with the NCB, and still sitting on the BSC Board of Directors, he was being billed as the other half of the British Heavyweight Championship along with Arthur Scargill.

Large redundancy payments had been the way in which Ian MacGregor had encouraged the steel industry to shed eighty five thousand of its workforce in just three years. Even larger payments, was the way in which he introduced yet another factor into the coal industry tempting miners to accept large financial inducements in exchange for their jobs. The union argued the jobs were not for the individual miner to sell, but they were the property of future generations living in the mining communities.

Arguments on both economic and moral grounds can be found to support the unions view. Although the NCB have said there would be no compulsory redundancies this promise could prove impossible to deliver. The British Steel Corporation made the same, but there were, whatever the claims to the contrary, reluctant volunteers.

It should be remembered that The Cumbria coalfield now has only one pit, North Wales, two and Kent just three. Pit closures would mean that there will come a time when redundant miners in these coalfields will have nowhere to go. A redundant miner who gets transferred away from his community would be faced with the various personal implications which go with such a decision. The uprooting of his family, who for one reason or another may be unable to move from their community. The family may also own or are in the process of buying their home in a community whose pit has just been closed, it is not hard to imagine the difficulty involved in selling a property before moving home. A miner faced with these problems may opt to accept the redundancy payment, but he could hardly be regarded as a volunteer. In taking the redundancy payment he then becomes a fair bet to join the long term unemployed. With unemployment in some mining areas now in excess of 20% it seems almost immoral to accept voluntary redundancy.

The transfer of miners from one pit to another also creates unemployment in both communities involved in the move. It could also be argued that the transfer of men from a colliery deemed "uneconomic" could have a detrimental effect on the future viability of the colliery or collieries which absorb the redundant workforce. The Rhondda Valley in South Wales provides such an example, where there were once more than fifty pits, just one, Maerdy Colliery now remains. Communities die as shops close and services are run down.

Unlike most redundancy schemes the NCB scheme would be Government funded. The scheme provides £1000 per year of service, to miners with over two years service. While the payments are well in excess of the statutory minimum provisions it should still be seen in context. Closing those pits which the NCB regard uneconomic would save the NCB's accounts £275 million annually, but the Government would loose £480 million per year in redundancy payments, unemployment benefits and lost tax revenue. Therefore, the cost to the Nations economy is much less than the cost of loosing the £475 million worth of coal produced by those pits.

The NCB's figures for pits are based on allocating costs and revenues by an arbitrary central formula, not on any assessment of actual investment in, and financial returns from individual pits. (These figures were calculated by the economist Andrew Glyn and supplied by the Labour Research Department in their booklet 'The Miners' Case.')

Closed pits means coal lost for everyone. Un-renewable assets are lost to the nation. The previous experience of running down the Coal Industry in the 1950's and 1960's turned out to be a disastrous mistake when oil prices soared in the 1970's. The other major factor was of course Margaret Thatcher and her Conservative government the overall employer of the public sector. With an impressive list of anti-trade union legislation under her belt and buffered by a large Parliamentary majority from the general election of June 9th 1983, when she became the first Tory Prime Minister, in the 20th Century, to win two consecutive elections, - and still enjoyed a remarkably high level of popularity.

The government had overseen defeats for trade unions in the public sector for the steelworkers, the health workers, the locomotive drivers' union ASLEF, British Leyland and the Civil Service. The government always recognised the potential industrial muscle of the NUM, Joe Gormley had led the miners to strike victories in 1972 and 1974, the latter had of course brought about the demise of Mr Edward Heath's Conservative government. 1974 saw the return to power of Harold Wilson's Labour government with Michael Foot as Employment Secretary. Mr Foot met with the NCB and the NUM and drew up the Plan for Coal which outlined that pit closures should only take place in cases of exhaustion, geological fault, or on safety grounds.

In 1972, the six day struggle to close the Saltley depot at Birmingham (the biggest coal stock pile in the country) saw the NUM victorious. Once closed the blockade of power stations was clinched. Saltley was closed by the use of some fifteen thousand Flying pickets, the police and government saw the need to rectify this. After 1972 the government set up a National Security Committee to review means of coping with similar emergencies - this was renamed the Civil Contingencies Committee by the Labour government in 1975. It is more than conjecture to assume that legislation by the Thatcher government which outlawed Secondary Picketing and improved police methods were inspired by

1972 and intended for use in any industrial dispute which posed a threat to the government. Without doubt policing had been radically updated as a result of the inner city riots of 1981 which had occurred at Bristol, Liverpool, Manchester and Brixton.

On the 27th May 1978 a leaked Tory policy group report drafted by Mr Nicholas Ridley MP appeared in the 'Economist' journal. It discussed setting financial targets for nationalised industries in preparation for privatisation.

Union resistance was anticipated with the coal industry pinpointed as the most likely battlefield. The report suggested that a future Conservative government should prepare for such a battle by:-

    (a) building up coal stocks at power stations.
    (b) plan for the import of foreign coal.
    (c) convert power stations to dual coal/oil firing.
    (d) encourage the employment of non-union labour by hauliers.
    (e) improve policing to deal with mass picketing.
    (f) make trade unions responsible for financing strikers.

This report was probably dusted down when Margaret Thatcher took office in May 1979. It is perhaps worth considering her appointment of Mr Peter Walker as energy secretary. Walker regarded as a wet, to borrow from the Tory vocabulary, had also been a member of Ted Heath's cabinet and therefore added quite a considerable axe to grind where miners were concerned.

Against this background the NUM embarked on a nineteen week overtime ban, which had been approved at their October 1983 conference, when a wage claim linked to the threat of a pit closures resolution was carried unanimously. During the ban several unrelated disputes flared up particularly in Yorkshire.

On March 6th 1984, Coal Board Chairman Ian MacGregor announced that the NCB's plans for the ensuing year included the reduction of twenty thousand jobs which would be cut across the country. This programme of job losses was interpreted to mean the closure of approximately twenty high cost collieries. The decimation of the British Steel Corporation had denied the NCB of it's biggest customer of coking coal, this coupled with geological faults in the South Wales coalfield meant that pits considered viable by the NCB, tended to be concentrated in the central coalfields. The NUM's argument was that many coalfields had been starved of investment and technology. Investment had been concentrated mainly in the viable areas i.e. high cost pits were created by deliberate Coal Board policy.

Another factor in determining the cost of coal production must be seen by the amount of subsidy the industry receives from the government compared with the NCB's foreign competitors. The union argued that the cost of closing 'unprofitable' pits outweighs the cost of keeping them open by the time redundancy payments and unemployment benefits are taking into account. Peter Walker gave the last figures available for comparison on subsidies from state financed capital investment.

1982,
    United Kingdom   £1.1 billion
    France   £347 million
    Belgium   £138 million
    West Germany   £62 million

Production costs and the direct level of subsidy by tonne, however, are as follows:-

1981/82,
    Belgium   £61
    West Germany   £47
    France   £45
    United Kingdom   £41

One of the pits named for closure by the NCB, was Cortonwood in South Yorkshire. The date for closure was fixed for April 6th 1984. Cortonwood had produced high quality coking coal from the Silkstone seam which fuelled the blast furnaces at Sheffield steelworks. Since October 1983 the NCB had opened two new faces on this seam. Local NCB officials concluded from a 1983 review that there was five years work left at the colliery. In fact miners from Elsecar Main Colliery had been transferred to Cortonwood. In any case the cost of coal extraction was found to be too high with an estimated loss of £20 per tonne and closure of the pit was announced. The NCB also earmarked four other pits for closure. These were Bullcliffe Wood (Yorkshire,) Herrington (Durham,) Polmaise (Scotland,) and Snowdown (Kent.)

On March 5th the Yorkshire NUM reacted by calling for strike action. Tuesday March 6th, the Scottish NUM followed suit. Rule 41 of the NUM constitution allows individual areas to call strikes so long as they have the backing of the National Executive. A ballot under rule 41 is not required, as it must be remembered the union at national level grew from the Miners' Federation of Great Britain. On the 8th March the National Executive met at Sheffield and gave the strikes the necessary backing. The NUM was now close to its first national strike since 1974.

Cortonwood was a microcosm of the threat to pits throughout the rest of the country and a national strike was imminent without a ballot relying on a domino effect coalfield by coalfield. It was, however, already anticipated that the leadership were taking a gamble as some moderate coalfields, Nottinghamshire being the prime example, were to be very reluctant dominoes.

SAVE THE PITS!

Week 1 - "Here We Go"

Monday March 12th, the 1984 miners' strike began facing a revolt even in the traditionally militant coalfields of Scotland and South Wales. Only Yorkshire and Kent were solidly behind the strike call. The revolt on day one in South Wales must have come as a personal blow to Area President Emlyn Williams as it was he who had proposed that individual areas should receive the unions backing at the National Executive meeting held the previous week. The strike call was rejected by sixteen South Wales pits and backed by only ten employing some six thousand, two hundred men. The revolt in Scotland centred, around Bilston Glen colliery at Loanhead, Midlothian which was the scene of mass picketing. In the North-East Durham supported, but Northumberland rejected. Leicestershire decided to work on. Nottinghamshire's position was to oppose a strike until a ballot to be held later in the week. Yorkshire Flying Pickets prevented the night shift at Nottinghamshire's Harworth colliery from clocking on. Ray Chadburn (Notts President) appealed to his Yorkshire counterpart Jack Taylor to keep his men away from Nottinghamshire until after their ballot had been held. Cumberland, Lancashire, Derbyshire, North Wales, the Midlands (Staffordshire and Warwickshire) were yet to decide.

A concerted effort by the South Wales leadership saw only six pits working by the night-shift. Mick McGahey Vice-President of the NUM predicted there would be a total national stoppage by the end of the week.

The second day of the strike left one hundred and four out of the one hundred and seventy four pits idle across the country, according to NCB assessments this meant 109,000 of the nation's 183,000 miners were involved in the stoppage. All but one of the pits in Nottinghamshire was being picketed. Flying pickets from Yorkshire numbering about two hundred and fifty confronted miners trying to clock on at Ollerton colliery, Notts. Using provisions under the legislation on secondary picketing the NCB applied for a High Court injunction to prevent the use of flying pickets by the Yorkshire area NUM. Henry Richardson General Secretary of the Notts NUM made renewed appeals to the Yorkshire leaders to withdraw pickets until his membership had balloted.

The National Union of Railwaymen, the locomotive drivers' union ASLEF, the Transport and General Workers Union and the National Union of Seamen all pledged support to the coal strike.

The next day March 14th, Ollerton colliery was the main flashpoint. Police stopped coach loads of pickets on the A1 leading from Yorkshire to Ollerton. According to reports running street battles took place in the Nottinghamshire mining village as pickets attempted to prevent local miners from clocking on and clashed with police and local youths.

The worst violence that had been witnessed in the first week of the dispute left one man dead and several injured. Mr David Jones aged 24 a Yorkshire miner employed at Ackton Hall colliery died in hospital after collapsing during the violent scenes at Ollerton. Pickets claimed he had been hit by a missile, but police said no violence was involved in Mr Jones' death. It was later confirmed that he died as a result of chest injuries, although at the subsequent inquest in Mansfield an open verdict was returned. Arthur Scargill appealed to all of his members to "behave responsibly" in the wake of the tragic death. Ian MacGregor said "It is sad that despite this tragic incident the pickets have still not been withdrawn."

Meanwhile production was halted at every pit in South Wales, although some men had attempted to cross picket lines.

Three coach loads of Kent miners were outnumbered by police in Leicestershire and so they failed to turn men away from work.

The Deputy Speaker of the House of Commons Mr Harold Walker was caught up in a controversy surrounding the NCB's application for a court injunction against the Yorkshire NUM, when he admitted that comments he had made on a radio interview were "Inconsistent with the political impartiality traditionally observed by the Deputy Speaker." Mr Walker had remarked that Ian MacGregor's decision to seek an injunction was "The daftest thing he has done since he took office."

On Thursday March 15th, the Home Secretary, Mr Leon Brittan set the tone for the role of the police in the dispute when he told the House of Commons that the police role would not necessarily be a passive one, "If they are attacked they will defend themselves" he further stated that police from all over the country were being mobilised "To ensure that any miner who wishes to work at any pit may do so and any miner who wishes to vote may do so." The Home Secretary also revealed that three thousand police officers from seventeen forces were on hand, he said the law permitted peaceful picketing "What it does not permit is what some Nottinghamshire miners themselves – who have been the victims of disgraceful conduct – have called mob rule." Brittan's hard line reflected the Prime Minister's anger at the inability of some Chief Constables to control mass picketing, she told the Commons, "Intimidation and violence must not win." Labour's Shadow Home Secretary Gerald Kaufmann told MPs "The government has a vested interest in provoking industrial anarchy. The Prime Minister has sown hatred and despair. I hope she is satisfied with what she has done."

There were more violent scenes in the Notts Coalfield at Thoresby colliery, urgent talks followed between the Executives of Yorkshire and Nottinghamshire these were attended by Arthur Scargill. Peace was restored to the coalfield after a decision by Nottinghamshire to stop work until after the result of their area ballot was known.

Elsewhere flying pickets from South Wales descended on the two North Wales pits of Bersham near Wrexham and Point of Ayr near Prestatyn. The first week of the strike ended as it had began with the leadership facing a revolt against a national strike. A massive no vote was returned from almost half of the British coalfields.

Nottinghamshire rejected the strike call by an overwhelming three votes to one. North Wales by two to one. The Midlands, South Derbyshire, Lancashire, Cumberland and the Durham mechanics all voted against the strike. Northumberland voted in favour of a strike, but fell 3% short of the 55% majority required for strike action under union rules, however, Mr Dennis Murphy area NUM President called for his men to strike. The British coalfield was now split with Scotland, Yorkshire, Durham, Kent and South Wales all solidly backing the dispute.

Once the results of the individual area ballots had been announced there were immediate calls for a national ballot and miners' leaders were coming under heavy pressure to call an immediate meeting of the National Executive. Trevor Bell the moderate leader of the unions' white-collar section COSA, said "It's time there was an immediately meeting of the Executive Committee to reconsider the strategy we decided upon at the last Executive Meeting. The real issue has been lost and we need to get public attention back to the problem facing us of closures and cuts in manpower. I'm hoping that someone in Head Office will reach the same conclusion." Nottinghamshire President Ray Chadburn claimed the outcome of his areas ballot would have been different without the picketing by the Yorkshire men, he said "If our members had been left alone the result would have been different. We failed to get our membership behind us because they have not believed us. But there will still be pit closures in Nottinghamshire and they will realise that what we have been saying all along is true."

Week 2 - A Paramilitary State

A massive police operation to curb the dispute being spread by flying pickets was mounted as the strike began its second week. The police operation was co-ordinated from a national reporting centre at New Scotland Yard, under the command of Mr David Hall of Humberside in his capacity as Chairman of the Chief Police Officers Association.

Thousands of pickets from Kent, South Wales and Yorkshire were prevented from converging on pits in coalfields that had voted to work. Pickets were being stopped and dispersed by the huge police presence on Britain's roads. This action quickly became the subject of controversy and the Kent leadership took legal advice with a view to seeking an injunction against the police. Sixteen car loads of Kent miners were stopped at the Dartford tunnel by what John Moyle (Betteshanger NUM) called "masses of police." The men were informed that they would be charged if they were caught outside the county. The National Council for Civil Liberties said the police were acting "Well outside their lawful authority." Miners in North Derbyshire were ordered out by their leaders, partly in protest against the massive police presence. Mr Dennis Skinner the Labour MP for Bolsover (himself a former President of Derbyshire NUM 1966-70) failed in a bid to get an emergency debate in the House of Commons claiming miners were being intimidated by the police activity.

The NUM leadership suffered a setback when a High Court Judge rejected the application by the Kent NUM for an injunction against the Chief Constable of Kent. Area President Malcolm Pitt said his members would continue to go into other coalfields as such action was "perfectly legal." On the other hand Yorkshire NUM must have been heartened with the news that the NCB had decided to suspend its court action against flying pickets.

The controversy over the policing of the dispute had already moved centre stage. Arthur Scargill said it was "absolutely appalling" that ten thousand police had been deployed in Nottinghamshire and Derbyshire preventing free movement of people, it was he added "a paramilitary state." Labour MPs took up the call at Question Time in the Commons where the Leader of the House Mr John Biffen was deputising for Margaret Thatcher who was in Brussels. John Biffen told the Commons "If a constable reasonably concludes that people are travelling to take part in a picket or circumstances where there is likely to be a breach of the peace, he has the common law power to call on them not to continue their journey." Mr Biffen denied that the government had plans to put armed forces on alert to deal with the dispute after being challenged by the Labour MP for Chesterfield Tony Benn. Another Labour member Tony Blair (Sedgefield) claimed the police had been given "arbitrary emergency powers."

Apart from the controversial policing, the call for a national ballot was the other main issue in the early days of the strike, as indeed it would continue to be. The issue gained momentum with a call from the Durham NUM, the first such call from a coalfield backing the strike. Leading the clamour for a ballot were the working miners, the coal board, the press, media and the Tory Party, not necessarily in that order.

The second week of the dispute also saw the rejection by steelworkers at Port Talbot in South Wales of a request by the area NUM to black Polish coking coal for steelmaking. The steelplants' blast furnace men voted unanimously against the NUM's plea as it was seen as a threat to their own jobs. So in many ways week two was setting the pattern for the rest of the coal strike.

As the week drew to a close, Lancashire leaders called out their men overturning a two to one decision against strike action, a rebellion seemed likely and the NCB called it an "abdication of democracy."

Representatives of Britain's seven thousand opencast workers at fifty four sites around the country decided that coal should not be moved from their workings. The TGWU who represent the opencast men said they would allow dispensation only for pensioners, the disabled, schools and hospitals.

Arthur Scargill, Jack Taylor and the Secretary of the Yorkshire NUM Owen Briscoe headed a column of miners at the funeral of Mr David Jones who was buried at South Kirkby, West Yorkshire. Attended by a large crowd, the police presence was discreet and among the floral tributes was one from the Chief Constable of Nottinghamshire.

It is indeed a sad irony that David Gareth Jones was not the first miner on strike from Ackton Hall colliery to lose his life. Now just a footnote in labour history, in 1893 James Gibbs and James Duggan were shot dead by troops sent to the pit to put down unrest. Whilst an open verdict was recorded in 1984 it is indisputable that following the reading of the Riot Act both Gibb and Duggan were killed by Dragoons 91 years before.

Week 3 - Coal vs Steel

Week three began with the centre of the stage dominated by the three major issues of the second week, i.e. steel, the police and the national ballot.

The steel unions at Scunthorpe were informed by BSC management that production would have to be scaled down as only two of their three blast furnaces were able to operate due to coal shortages. A spokesman for the corporation said other steel plants had adequate coal stocks for the time being.

Ken Toon the moderate leader of the South Derbyshire NUM claimed that his call to Arthur Scargill to convene a meeting of the national executive to discuss a national ballot had been neither answered nor acknowledged.

The Vice-President of the South Wales NUM Terry Thomas called for an independent inquiry into a press report that members of the armed forces dressed as police officers were being used on picket line duty in the central coalfields.

Men at Bersham colliery in North Wales refused to cross the South Wales flying picket line, and had now joined the strike. But the only other pit in the area, Point of Ayr was producing coal with its miners crossing the picket line. Heavy picketing by Yorkshiremen continued despite the large police operation in Nottinghamshire.

Frustration at the way police in Derbyshire were preventing miners joining the picket lines brought a new dimension to the dispute when two hundred men were stopped and turned back. Prevented from approaching Creswell colliery they abandoned some fifty vehicles on the M1 motorway. Police quickly restored order after fighting broke out between pickets and drivers of other vehicles using the motorway. One policeman required hospital treatment. A police spokesman said "This was a deliberate attempt, danger to life cannot be justified." Despite the attentions of the police some five hundred pickets eventually massed at Creswell colliery, where there were four arrests. Daw Mill colliery in Warwickshire was also the scene of some considerable action mostly involving flying pickets from South Wales, a policeman was taken to hospital with rib injuries during clashes with two hundred strikers.

A call from Jack Collins Secretary of the Kent NUM for "a total power stoppage" was met with a huge deployment of flying pickets to Britain's power stations trying to put a stranglehold on the electricity network.

The NUM picket line at Port Talbot steelworks was reinforced by nurses and health workers from South Wales hospitals. The members of the National Union of Public Employees were taking part in reciprocal action for the assistance the NUM had given to the health workers.

A joint meeting between Arthur Scargill and the General Secretaries of six other unions laid plans to black the movement of coal and coke throughout Britain. Leaders of sea, rail, and road transport took part as did Bill Sirs of the Iron and Steel Trades Confederation, who pledged his full support – later events were to prove this would not be forthcoming. The other General Secretaries who took part in this top level meeting were Moss Evans (TGWU,) Ray Buckton (ASLEF,) Jimmy Knapp (NUR,) Jim Slater (NUS,) and Bert Lyons (Transport Salaried Staff Association.) After the meeting Scargill said, "I am absolutely delighted with the assistance that has been offered. I am quite certain it will strengthen the resolve of miners currently involved in the dispute."

In what many people in the Labour movement would recognise as a predictable move, Bill Sirs staged an about turn, saying he would not support the miners if it affected jobs in the steel industry. "I am not here to see the steel industry crucified on someone else's altar." Dealing a savage blow to the so-called 'Triple Alliance' between the coal, steel and rail unions, Sirs' change of heart came in response to the unease of steel-men at Ravenscraig, Scunthorpe and the outcome of a meeting between South Wales NUM Leaders with the unions of Llanwern and Port Talbot who said they intended to continue working normally. Mr Sirs' statement was echoed by Mr Bob Haslam BSC Chairman, who while speaking at Scunthorpe said, "Not to put too fine a point on it we are in danger of being damaged by conflict in our sister industry which appears not yet to have faced up to its current structural problems in the way the steel industry has had to do. One wonders whether the miners themselves recognise they too are in danger of loosing permanently even more of their future market if the steel industry is damaged by their actions in this way." Depending on your point of view Mr Haslam's remarks could be seen as one of genuine concern for the industry he heads, or an attempt by a leading member of British management to cause division between the coal miner and the steelworker.

Lancashire Area NUM delegates met at Bolton and decided to recommend a return to work after they had called their members out for a week to allow some breathing space following heavy picketing by Yorkshire men. The moderate leader of Lancashire Sid Vincent who had originally backed the strike said his area was split down the middle and that the situation could only be resolved by holding a national ballot.

It was a bright cold day in April, and the clocks were striking thirteen.
George Orwell, "1984," first sentence.

Week 4 - Flashpoint - Port Talbot

The row surrounding the call for a national ballot reached the House of Commons when Energy Secretary Mr Peter Walker made the call whilst answering a question from Tony Benn Labour MP for Chesterfield, and himself a former Energy Secretary. Benn had asked for a statement on energy supplies, Walker replied that there was enough coal to last six months and then said he hoped that the NUM would ballot. The Speaker Mr Bernard Weatherill, remonstrated with Peter Walker for broadening the scope of the question.

Miners in Lancashire braved the picket lines and returned to work. Agecroft colliery was in full production but two pits Sutton Manor and Bold, both near St Helens, decided to stay out and their men joined picket lines in other parts of the coalfield.

Tuesday April 3rd, there were eleven arrests outside Port Talbot steelworks when four hundred striking miners tried to prevent the movement of coke. One miner was knocked unconscious and there were complaints of police violence and claims that the police had charged into the miners' ranks, a police spokesman said "All we were doing was allowing free passage for lorries and cars."

Margaret Thatcher joined the call for national ballot "I am concerned that the miners should have a chance to express their views on their right to go to their place of work and earn a decent living," she told the House of Commons.

Wednesday April 4th, there were more angry clashes between strikers and police outside Port Talbot steelworks, there were six arrests as the pickets action was intensified by the arrival at the plant's deep water harbour of a Norwegian ship laden with 60,000 tonnes of Australian coal. A spokesman for BSC said the picketing was having only a minimal effect.

Trade and Industry Secretary Mr Norman Tebbitt who had cultivated a reputation for abrasive remarks told a press conference of parliamentary journalists "I just wonder whether we would have a coal mining dispute if we had denationalised the coal industry ten or twenty years ago. I fancy we would probably have cheaper coal, cheaper electricity, better paid miners and a more efficient economy today. It is a thought, is it not, for the future."

Thursday April 5th, for the third day running Port Talbot was the main flashpoint of the dispute when six hundred miners clashed with two hundred police resulting in thirty nine arrests. Ray Powell MP (Labour-Ogmore) witnessed the clashes in which pickets tried to overturn a police van and described the policing as "over-zealous."

In the House of Commons the Leader of the Opposition Mr Neil Kinnock announced that the Shadow Home Secretary Mr Gerald Kaufmann would be calling for an emergency debate on the dispute.

Friday April 6th, the week of confrontation at Port Talbot cooled considerably, but there were two arrests taking the total for the week to fifty eight.

Week 5 - Flashpoint – Sheffield

The South Wales area NUM took the initiative to defuse the potentially dangerous picket line at Port Talbot. Hoping the police would follow their lead they decided to reduce the number of pickets to a minimum. Area President Emlyn Williams said "I don't want to see someone killed or badly injured on a picket line." The move was welcomed by the police. But in North Wales relations between police and pickets became the subject of fresh controversy when the North Wales Chief Constable Mr David Owen admitted "It is part of my policy to deploy plain clothes officers with a view to identifying persons responsible for committing offences." The Chief Constable's admission that he had used detectives on the picket line confirmed allegations made by miners from Point of Ayr colliery.

In other parts of the British coalfield the picket line confrontation continued. Two thousand pickets outnumbered police at Babbington colliery in Nottinghamshire and following scuffles there were over sixty arrests and six policemen were injured. At Silverdale colliery in Staffordshire the Midlands General Secretary Jim Colgan was arrested. Both the President and Vice-President of the Derbyshire NUM Austin Fairest and Peter Elliot were arrested outside Creswell colliery.

The Speaker of the House of Commons Mr Bernard Weatherill, granted an application by Barnsley Labour MP Mr Allen McKay, for a three hour emergency debate – this was the seventh application since the beginning of the strike.

At BSC Llanwern two coal trains were allowed into the works as part of an agreement which had been reached between the South Wales NUM and the steel unions.

Thursday April 12th, the long awaited meeting of the National Executive took place at the NUM headquarters in Sheffield. Few people could have predicted the events which took place both inside and outside the union's HQ in a multi-storey office block, St James' House in the city centre. Scuffles broke out when placard waving demonstrators surged forward as the Executive members arrived for their crucial meeting, moderate leaders received a hostile reception from the crowd, the worst jostling was reserved for the Nottinghamshire leaders - Ray Chadrurn and Henry Richardson. Eleven policemen were hurt, five requiring hospital treatment. Two demonstrators were also injured and fifty three were arrested as the three thousand miners clashed with twelve hundred police in ranks six deep. At one stage Arthur Scargill appeared at a seventh floor window and criticised the massive police presence using a loud-hailer to make himself heard.

Inside the Executive meeting a move by Leicestershire leader Jack Jones to call for a national ballot was quickly ruled out of order by Arthur Scargill who was of course presiding. Instead it was agreed to convene a special delegates' conference for a weeks time. The conference would decide the direction of the dispute and to consider a possible rule change to the NUM constitution. The rule change would allow a simple majority in a ballot for strike action replacing the 55% majority requirement.

After the meeting Arthur Scargill defended his controversial ruling on the national ballot question saying that the proposal directly opposed the unanimous decision taken by the Executive meeting held on March 8th allowing each area the right to call individual strikes. Addressing a delighted crowd of miners he said the NUM were even more determined to continue "The fight against Thatcher and MacGregor on pit closures." The crowd responded by singing "we'll support you evermore," one of the strike anthems.

In the House of Commons, the Prime Minister denounced the Executive's decision, she said "Many miners will be greatly concerned that the chance for a national ballot has been delayed still further." Her comments were directed at Opposition leader Neil Kinnock. The miners' strike was seen by the Government as an issue with which to embarrass the Labour Party Leadership.

Mr Kinnock was coming under continual pressure to call for a national ballot and to denounce picket line violence. Kinnock had enjoyed his fair share of popularity since being elected Labour Party Leader in October of 1983, and the party itself appeared to be recovering well from the rout it had received from the Tories at the June 1983 General Election, when it had returned only two hundred and nine MPs to Parliament.

To the government the miners' strike presented them with the ideal political opportunity of ending Neil Kinnock's 'Honeymoon.'

> *Hell, there are no rules here - we're trying to accomplish something.*
> Thomas A Edison.

Week 6 - The Rule Change

The Prime Minister set up a special inner cabinet to monitor the dispute, the team of ministers were Mr Peter Walker (Energy,) Mr Norman Tebbitt (Trade and Industry,) Mr Tom King (Employment,) Sir Michael Havers (Attorney General,) Mr David Mitchell (Transport,) Mr Michael Ancram (Scottish Office,) Mr Douglas Hurd (Home Office) and Lord Trefgarne (Under Secretary for the Armed Forces.) The appointment of Lord Trefgarne gave rise to much comment and conjecture and the Shadow Energy Secretary Mr Stan Orme said that his inclusion was symptomatic of Mrs Thatcher's bunker mentality."

The Labour MP for Sunderland North, Bob Clay, was arrested outside a privately owned opencast mine at Deerness in Co Durham. His personal assistant said he had witnessed "shocking scenes" at the picket line and that he had seen one man "badly beaten by police." Mr Clay appeared before Bishop Auckland Magistrates' court with fifteen other pickets.

At the Scottish TUC, two of the top union leaders made calls for Government intervention to bring the NCB and the NUM together for talks. Terry Duffy, President of the AUEW said "If the Government does not do this the consequences will be catastrophic for our nation." The TUC chairman Ray Buckton (ASLEF) also called for talks to end the strike. Delegates approved a proposition to call a one day stoppage in Scotland in support of the NUM. Ian MacGregor poured cold water on the calls for negotiations by saying that meeting Arthur Scargill was "not a constructive way" to spend his time. The war of words was taken up by Mr Scargill who accused Mr MacGregor of being the Government's agent in the dispute.

Five South Wales miners from Cwm colliery, Beddau were arrested for distributing union leaflets on a Nottinghamshire housing estate and were charged under a section of the Public Order Act which covers the distribution of threatening, obscene or insulting literature. The offending leaflet headed - "A Strike Breaker is a Traitor," showed a photograph of police escorting blacklegs in the Garw valley, South Wales in 1929, the leaflet also carried Jack London's "Definition Of A Scab." On the reverse side the arguments in favour of the coal strike were outlined and a South Wales NUM imprint was included at the bottom of the leaflet. NUM officials asked Labour MPs to investigate the arrests.

On Thursday April 19th, the special delegate conference was held at Sheffield Memorial Hall. A noisy rally was held outside and was attended by some seven thousand demonstrators. Inside the conference the crucial motion for the rule change was proposed by Arthur Scargill. He was opposed by Mr Roy Lynk of Nottinghamshire one of the delegation representing an area where the majority of the thirty four thousand miners were still working. Earlier in the week the Area Council of the Nottinghamshire NUM had decided by a massive four to one against the rule change. There had even been calls for the resignation of their leaders prompting Ray Chadburn to say "We are being alienated from the rest of the British Trade Union movement. We are once again requesting our members that they should support the national union." When put to the vote the conference approved the rule change by 187,000 votes to 59,000. It now looked as if Scargill had removed the last obstacle for calling and winning a national ballot although it was soon to become clear that this was not to be his tactics and in the long term to prove an error of judgement.

The delegate conference also gave the national leadership i.e. Arthur Scargill, Vice-President Mick McGahey and General Secretary Peter Heathfield direct responsibility for the day to day running of the dispute and the authority to call the forty five thousand miners still working to join the stoppage. After the conference, Nottinghamshire General Secretary Henry Richardson declared "We are calling on everyone to come out on strike – we are calling for Trade Unionism now."

Friday April 20th, Mr Heathfield told a twelve hundred strong rally at Port Talbot that the decisions of the delegate conference had given the dispute a true national character. He said it was the duty of every miner to fight against pit closures "It is our turn to carry the banners to preserve what those who have gone before us have achieved."

The response from the NCB was the announcement by Ian MacGregor that the board would launch an advertising campaign to persuade miners to ignore the NUM's call for national strike action. The chairman accused Arthur Scargill of using lies and intimidation to perpetuate the six week old dispute.

'A Strike-breaker is a traitor'

Blacklegs in the Garw Valley of South Wales in 1929.

Jack London's definition of a Scab.

'After God had finished the rattlesnake, the toad and vampire, He had some awful substance left with which he made a scab.

'A scab is a two-legged animal with a cork-screw soul, a water-logged brain, a combination backbone of jelly and glue. Where others have a heart, he carries a tumour of rotten principles.

'When a scab comes down the street, men turn their backs, the angels weep in heaven, and the Devil shuts the gates of Hell to keep him out.

'No man has a right to scab so long as there is a pool of water to drown his carcass in, or a rope long enough to hang his body with. Judas Iscariot was a gentleman compared with a scab, for after betraying his Master he had character enough to hang himself. A scab has not.

'Esau sold his birthright for a mess of pottage. Judas Iscariot sold his Saviour for 30 pieces of silver. Benedict Arnold sold his country for the promise of a commission in the British Army. The modern strike-breaker sells his birthright, his country, his wife, his children and his fellow-men for an unfilled promise from his employer.

'Esau was a traitor to himself; Judas Iscariot was a traitor to his God; Benedict Arnold was a traitor to his country. A STRIKE-BREAKER IS A TRAITOR to his God, his country, his wife, his family and his class. A REAL MAN NEVER BECOMES A STRIKE-BREAKER . . . .'

Week 7 – Hardship Funds

Following the Easter Holidays it was time to see whether the working miners would now heed the leadership's call and join the strike or if they continued to work, whether or not the police would be able to ensure their safe passage through the picket lines.

In the House of Commons the Energy Under Secretary Mr Giles Shaw rejected calls from the opposition benches for Government intervention, he informed MPs that there were pits working in Nottinghamshire, Leicestershire, Warwickshire, Staffordshire and parts of Lancashire, Derbyshire, Cumbria and North Wales. "This means that over thirty five thousand men in over forty collieries will again today demonstrate their readiness to continue working," he said. Shadow energy spokesman Mr Stan Orme said it was the government's responsibility to resolve the strike and Liberal energy spokesman Mr Alan Beith called upon the government to bring the two sides together.

A meeting of the Labour Party National Executive called on its constituency parties to levy fifty pence per week from it's total membership to support the NUM strike fund and prevent the government starving the miners back to work. The Labour controlled Local Authorities throughout the country and the Trade Unions were giving various financial support and other aid to the miners. Soup kitchens and Hardship Funds were being set up throughout the British coalfields and beyond. As in no previous industrial dispute the role of women was a prominent one, Womens' Support Groups were established in virtually every mining village in the country. The concept of women giving support in a strike, was in itself no new thing, in fact you can read in R Page Arnot's 'South Wales Miners' of the quaintly named 'Committee of Lady Helpers' as far back as 1912, however the women of 1984 (by no means exclusively miners' wives) were to be found on demonstrations and on the picket line as well as running the food kitchens. Financial hardship always the enemy of the striker, had become more acute as a result of government legislation which deemed that unions paid £15 strike pay to it's members, in the case of the NUM the strike pay was theoretical.

The appeal for financial aid was taken up by Arthur Scargill, speaking at a rally in Northumberland, he said "We will ask every British Trade Union member to contribute fifty pence a week to our hardship fund. The money will enable our members to go on living instead of just surviving," turning his attention to the divided Nottinghamshire coalfield and the police presence there he said a demonstration was planned," We want thousands there. We will walk into Nottinghamshire. If that means we shall all get arrested, then we shall all get arrested." The leader of the Social Democrats Dr David Owen MP for Plymouth-Devonport criticised the organising of a rally in Nottinghamshire, he said Scargill was determined to get himself arrested so that he could fight the dispute from behind prison bars.

Week seven ended with a rallying call from Arthur Scargill to a ten thousand strong crowd at Sophia Gardens Cardiff. He was joined on the platform by Mick McGahey and Emlyn Williams together with Ray Buckton (ASLEF,) Jimmy Thomas (NUR) and George Henderson (TGWU) whose construction section represents workers in opencast mining. Strikers from working pits in Nottinghamshire and from Point of Ayr colliery, North Wales were given standing ovations as they took their place in the column before the march set off, in brilliant sunshine from the Civic Centre.

At the rally Arthur Scargill repeated his call for a massive turnout at the Nottinghamshire demonstration and he paid tribute to the South Wales miners "To the miners of South Wales I say a heartfelt thank you for the tremendous way you are fighting. I salute you for what you have done and what you will do. Make no mistake in months and years to come all of us in this movement will look back in pride when faced with a government whose only weapon is destruction, we stood and fought not only for the right to work, to save jobs and pits, but to retain our self-respect and dignity as human beings." Mick McGahey said he hoped that Wales TUC would follow the example of the Scottish TUC in calling for a one day stoppage in support of the miners.

Week 8 – The Triple Alliance

Mr Roy Hattersley the Deputy Leader of the Labour Party threw his weight behind the dispute on ITV's 'Weekend World' television programme. Mr Hattersley said there were ideological differences not only between Mr Scargill and himself but also between Mr Scargill and his own membership. "But this argument, this battle, this strike is not an ideological strike" he said "This strike is about the coal industry there is very little difference between Mr Scargill and me about the future of the coal industry, about the need to preserve our energy supplies, for the government to carry out proper industrial relations rather than industrial relations by diktat." Mr Hattersley went on to say he believed a ballot would have been the right thing, but, "It is an official strike by any standards" he said, adding "If I were a Nottingham miner I would be on strike."

Jack Taylor told a big May Day rally at Doncaster "I am confident that sooner or later the Nottingham men will be persuaded to come into line, but make no mistake about it the cost of their defiance has been enormous both financially and in terms of morale."

Arthur Scargill addressed a meeting attended by about seven hundred people at Sutton-in-Ashfield, Nottinghamshire, his third visit to the coalfield within a week in an attempt to persuade the working miners to join the strike.

The issue of Coal versus Steel reared it's head again with a bitter attack on the NUM by Mr Clive Lewis the ISTC Scottish officer. Reacting to a decision by the Triple Alliance (coal, steel and rail unions) taken at a meeting in Edinburgh the previous week to halve the amount of coal to be allowed into Ravenscraig steelworks, he said that the action would end production at the works and could cause permanent closure. "The NUM are favouring the Welsh plants" he said. The allegation by Mr Lewis was denied by Welsh union leaders who said Port Talbot was receiving foreign coal through it's deep water harbour which the NUM could not prevent and that Llanwern was in exactly the same position as Ravenscraig.

Neil Kinnock followed Roy Hattersley in backing the miners. Speaking on BBC TV he said "It is time all miners joined the strike" but he stressed "I really don't believe that unless and until, a national ballot comes the strike will have widespread effect. Therefore the action which I support to defend the industry will not have the effect intended." The Labour Leadership and Mr Kinnock in particular had been under pressure from the miners and the rank and file of the Labour movement to give the strike full support.

At Mansfield working Nottinghamshire miners held an anti-strike rally outside the area NUM HQ. There was trouble as over fifteen hundred strikers from other coalfields told their working colleagues, that they were betraying their union. Mr

Henry Richardson told his Notts men "You're the only friends Ian MacGregor has got; it's about time you acted like bloody men and showed solidarity with other miners." During the demonstration mounted police battled to keep the rival factions apart and they made more than twenty arrests.

During the week there was trouble at Littleton colliery Staffordshire where two days running the police made a total of thirty two arrests as flying pickets attempted to prevent working miners from going in. There were also arrests outside another Staffordshire pit – Hem Heath colliery.

At the normally quiet Essex port of Wivenhoe, there were clashes between police and pickets as miners tried to prevent imported coal from leaving the port. Tuesday May 1st, a total of one hundred and seven arrests were made outside the non-union port as trouble flared. Wednesday 2nd May, the miners staged a sit down protest at the dock gates.

Arrests were made outside Ravenscraig steelworks when the BSC decided to transport desperately needed coal from Hunterston docks sixty miles away to the works by road. This was the BSC response to the Tripe Alliance decision to halve the plant's coal allocation. Police outnumbered pickets by three to one at times as the lorry convoys made their deliveries to the plant. Mick McGahey was present on the picket line where the arrests totalled fifteen. ASLEF responded to the BSC's emergency action by announcing that the last delivery had been made to the steel plant by rail in retaliation against the corporation's strike breaking tactics. Under the Triple Alliance agreement one trainload of coal would be delivered instead of two, it was estimated that ninety two lorry loads was the equivalent of one trainload.

A week which had also seen confrontation at Harworth colliery, Nottinghamshire where there were twenty one arrests and at Golbourne colliery Lancashire where there were eight arrests as over a thousand flying pickets brought the pit to a standstill, ended on a high note for the NUM Llandudno, North Wales. The Wales TUC annual conference unanimously backed an emergency resolution calling for a day of action. Emlyn Williams proposing the emergency motion said of Mrs Thatcher "We are going to defy her, we are not going back, we are going to fight and fight again. If we destroy her we are doing it for our class, the working class." The Wales TUC decision was in line with the one already made by the Scottish TUC.

Week 9 - Flashpoint – Ravenscraig

The three haulage firms which made up the Hunterston to Ravenscraig coal convoy had warned their drivers that unless they accepted the coal run there would be no alternative work. Ironically because the NUM had been supported by the rail unions in stopping the coal trains to Ravenscraig, the steelworks were now counting on the lorry drivers to ignore the recommendation of their union the TGWU, just as the drivers did in 1980 when the steelworks themselves were on strike.

The scene was set for confrontation and on Monday May 7th, one thousand pickets lined up against five hundred police outside the Motherwell plant. Amid ugly scenes there were thirty one arrests and one policeman was taken to hospital. Mick McGahey who was present said the picket line would be reinforced by men from the north of England.

Meanwhile Arthur Scargill addressed a rally at Mansfield asking the Notts miners to join the stoppage.

Tuesday May 8th, as South Wales cokemen reached agreement between the NUM and the BSC on supplies to the Llanwern steelworks the unions' knot on Ravenscraig was tightened. The TGWU said they would prevent fuel supplies reaching one of the haulage firms involved in the strike breaking convoy. Tugboatmen decided to black shops leaving and entering the Hunterston terminal. Violence flared on the picket line as about one hundred pickets tried to break through the police cordon when thirty seven lorries entered Hunterston after delivering coal to Ravenscraig. Five miners were taken to hospital after being trampled by police horses. Fighting between police and pickets led to sixty five arrests. The picket line, however, failed to stop the convoy.

Mr Bob Haslam the BSC chairman again intervened in the dispute when he said "It seems an unbelievable policy to deliberately try to drive steel out of business thus cutting its demand for coal permanently."

The Scottish Day of Action went ahead and Scotland's largest newspaper 'The Daily Record' failed to appear when it's editor refused to carry a pro-NUM statement from the print union SOGAT 82 on its front page.

Back at Ravenscraig steelworks six coach loads of miners were prevented from approaching the plant. The men retaliated with a sit down protest which in turn led to two hundred and ninety arrests as the police cleared the road.

At a meeting of the NUM national Executive the continuation of the strike was re-affirmed and the union's annual conference was cancelled saving the NUM an estimated £100,000.

Week 10 - Flashpoint - Mansfield

Week ten began with the arrest of thirty two Kent miners at Ramsgate Harbour. The pickets were trying to prevent a tanker unloading 3,000 tonnes of fuel oil to be used at the nearby Richborough power station which feeds the national grid. Kent NUM General Secretary Jack Collins said "The arrests will only strengthen the resolve of Kent miners in their strike. Other miners arrested last week had very restrictive bail conditions imposed when they appeared in court. If the courts try to impose the same bail conditions this time I think mineworkers should question the acceptance of such conditions." It had become a practise, during the strike, for magistrates to impose various restrictive bail conditions. They varied in severity from area to area and were becoming increasingly restrictive as the strike went on. A reason given was that the volume of arrests was too great for the courts to expeditiously process. The sort of conditions being imposed varied from bailed not to join an NUM picket line to bailees being subject to a curfew or being placed under virtual house arrest. By the use of these bail conditions the numbers on the picket line could be significantly reduced. Among the Kent miners arrested was Malcolm Pitt the NUM's Kent President. Pitt contrary to his bail conditions later joined a picket line at a coal depot at West Drayton, London.

The mass rally which Arthur Scargill had called for in Nottinghamshire was held at Mansfield and was attended by some fifteen thousand supporters. After the rally trouble flared in the town centre as the demonstrators were dispersing. Police made eighty eight arrests and forty of their number were injured. Fifty seven of those arrested were subsequently charged at a special court at Mansfield with various offences including assault, threatening behaviour, obstruction and possession of an offensive weapon. All were charged "That with others on May 14th at Mansfield they riotously assembled contrary to common law." One bail condition imposed was that they should not visit Nottinghamshire until their cases were to be heard on July 26th. Mr Charles McLachlan the chief constable of Nottinghamshire said "What took place went far beyond public order offences into something far more serious," he went on "Increasingly over the past two or three weeks we have seen a number of people appearing at Nottinghamshire pits, particularly from outside the county and an increase in levels of violence and intimidation. "Large numbers of people at pits can of themselves be intimidatory. It must be remembered that peaceful persuasion is all that is allowed by law. But when you add instances of arson, intimidation against wives and families, criminal damage to houses and vehicles and clear tactics which are designed to terrorise respectable working people in their own communities, we have gone a long way down a very sad road." This outspoken statement by the most beleaguered chief constable involved in policing the strike was on the surface quite fair, it fell short, however, by failing to explain why the right of peaceful persuasion was not in fact being allowed by the police and this often caused frustration which led to violence on the picket line.

The Secretary of State for Wales Mr Nicholas Edwards was attacked by miners when he visited the British Telecom factory at Cwmcarn, Gwent. The eighty miners agreed to withdraw after inflicting damage to the ministerial car, when Mr Edwards agreed to meet lodge officials from the North Celenyn and South Celenyn collieries, Newbridge. The meeting with a cabinet minister was hailed as a victory by NUM officials. There were no arrests. Elsewhere in South Wales forty women staged a peaceful picket outside Port Talbot steelworks.

Two Notts NUM branches - namely Pye Hill No 1 and Sherwood issued writs against the area's representatives on the national executive, to try to force the union to rescind its official support for the dispute.

Other events in what was a hectic week saw former NCB chairman Lord Ezra call for a national ballot in the House of Lords. Whilst in the commons, Mrs Thatcher again rejected calls for government intervention.

A Scottish Dock strike was averted after five hours of talks. The docks strike had been threatened by the TGWU after the ISTC had ignored a blacking order and unloaded coal destined for Ravenscraig at Hunterston.

Wednesday May 16th, Mrs Ann Scargill was one of eight women arrested at Silverhill colliery, Nottinghamshire. Mrs Scargill was charged with obstructing a free passageway and obstructing a police officer, she was bailed not to picket in Nottinghamshire during the dispute at a special hearing in Mansfield. Arthur Scargill said "Along with other women my wife was arrested on the picket line this morning while trying to persuade Nottinghamshire miners to join our fight to save pits and jobs. I am proud of her involvement and of the role that all the women support groups are playing in this dispute."

Labour Energy spokesman Stan Orme announced he was to meet both Mr Scargill and Mr MacGregor in an effort to stimulate talks to bring about an end to the dispute.

Week 11 - Conciliatory Tone

Mr Len Murray, the General Secretary of the TUC, who had previously announced his intention to retire from office in the Autumn, (one of his few inspirational decisions in recent years) came under attack from Trade Unionists after writing to the Yorkshire and Humberside Regional TUC criticising plans to call a one day stoppage in support of the miners. A similar letter was sent to the Wales TUC pointing out that the regions were exceeding their powers. Jim Slater the General Secretary of the National Union of Seamen said Mr Murray should get out of Congress House and see what was going on. The seaman's leader added that the north and south were now two different nations. Despite Murray's intervention the Yorkshire and Humberside action went ahead with bus stoppages at Doncaster and Barnsley, some rail disruption and sympathy action by one thousand Humberside dockers.

The leader of the Lancashire miners Sid Vincent, announced that working miners in his area would be disciplined under the NUM's Rule 35, Lancashire's twelve man executive took the decision viewing the contravention of a national instruction and conference decision as a serious offence. In accordance with Rule 35 the working miners would be suspended from membership for five years. "We hope it might bring them round to our way of thinking. The fight we are fighting is their fight as well," said Vincent. Miners at Lancashire's Agecroft colliery where the majority were working took out a High Court injunction to prevent the area NUM from imposing the suspension.

Kent leader Malcolm Pitt was again arrested on the picket line at Richborough power station and was remanded in custody for one week by Ramsgate magistrates.

Wednesday May 23rd, and the talks which Stan Orme had assisted in arranging were held at Hobart House, the NCB's London headquarters, but abandoned after just sixty five minutes. The talks attended by the NUM national executive ended with each side blaming the other for the breakdown. Mr Scargill claimed the meeting had been a fiasco and that the coal board chairman had treated the executive with contempt. Mr MacGregor said that Mr Scargill had been aggressive and contentious and unwilling to discuss the situation intelligently. Scargill's version was confirmed by every executive member without exception. Later the NCB adopted a more conciliatory attitude by writing to the union inviting it for talks on the 'Plan for Coal' and the industry's future. In the letter the NCB Deputy chairman Mr James Cowan suggested that in future talks should be conducted with both sides using a three man negotiating committee. The union agreed to meet for further talks on this basis and said their committee would be their three national officers Messrs Scargill, McGahey and Heathfield.

Following the collapse of the first pit talks Ian MacGregor had received a bad press and he offered to stand down from the rearranged meeting. This mood was reflected by the way in which the new talks were welcomed by the Prime Minister in Parliament, adopting a conciliatory tone she said, "I most earnestly hope that the talks will succeed because the government has done it's part in providing for investment in the future of the coal industry."

The sudden change of attitude by the board and the government seemed to stem from MacGregor's bad press and the fear of pushing public opinion in the miners' favour.

There were seven arrests outside Trawsfynedd nuclear power station in North Wales. A total of fifty eight arrests were made during the week at various pits in the Nottinghamshire coalfield. The week ended with a setback for the NUM when the High Court Judge Sir Robert Megarry ruled in favour of the Pye Hill and Sherwood Notts Miners who wanted the official strike call ruled unlawful.

Elsewhere on the increasingly complex industrial scene, the rail unions the NUR and ASLEF accepted a wage increase of 4.9% to 5.6%, thereby averting a national overtime ban. The National union of Seamen called a midweek stoppage of ferries for the following week as part of it's campaign against the government's plans to privatise 'Sealink'.

Week 12 - Flashpoint – Orgreave

The rescheduled talks and all the other events during the twelfth week of the strike were overshadowed by the unprecedented scenes outside the Orgreave coke plant near Rotherham South Yorkshire. Following two embarrassing defeats for pickets at the plant Arthur Scargill called for an army of flying pickets to stop coke convoys leaving the plant for Scunthorpe steelworks. Firstly, on the previous Friday May 25th, saw one thousand miners at the wrong gate when coke from Orgreave arrived at Scunthorpe steelworks through the back gate. Monday May 28th, one thousand pickets waited for coke to leave the plant while 6,000 tonnes of coal was sent in by another route. The Polish coal arrived via a wharf partly owned by the BSC on the River Trent and along a three mile route sealed off by police.

Tuesday May 29th, Arthur Scargill's call for a mass blockade of the coke works was answered when an estimated seven thousand pickets attempted to prevent the lorry convoys leaving the plant. The troubles began when thirty five lorries, protected by wire mesh arrived at the plant to load up. The hostile response was a barrage of missiles.

Mounted police supported by police in riot gear and carrying riot shields moved in to make arrests. One police officer suffered a broken leg when he fell from his horse as running skirmishes spilled into fields near the plant. Teams of ambulance men wearing helmets assisted the injured in scenes which resembled a battlefield. A strong police cordon then forced the crowd back as the first laden convoy emerged bound for Scunthorpe.

Approximately three hours later the convoy returned. Missiles rained on the police lines, once more the pickets scattered into the fields while mounted police again supported officers in riot gear. Fighting continued while the convoy of lorries were being reloaded. As the lorries left the police lines were again pelted, but the coke convoy got through. The police withdrew and then the mounted police charged, applauded by other officers. The huge police operation numbered some seventeen hundred officers deployed from thirteen forces, thirty seven police were reportedly injured as were twenty seven pickets, the police made eighty two arrests.

The police alleged that violence erupted when Scargill himself arrived at the plant, but Scargill said "What you have now in South Yorkshire is an actual police state tantamount to something you are used to seeing in Chile or Bolivia. We have seen riot shields and riot gear in action. We have seen truncheons and staves in action. We have seen mounted police officers charging into our ranks. I saw truncheons wielded and I saw our people hit. I saw people punched on the ground." Mr Scargill called on the whole trade union movement to respond. The Assistant Chief Constable of South Yorkshire defended his police action saying the use of riot gear, police dogs and mounted police was a "Deployment of last resort."

Wednesday May 30th, at Orgreave three thousand pickets clashed with two thousand police. Arthur Scargill was arrested and charged with obstructing the highway. The NUM President appeared later at Rotherham Magistrates court and was given unconditional bail until July 10th. He received a rapturous welcome from supporters waiting outside.

During his absence from the picket line the police made thirty five arrests, twenty four people were hurt in the violent clashes. A portable building was dragged across the road by pickets and set on fire. The assistant Chief Constable Mr Tony Clement blamed the picket line violence on drink and political infiltration, "People were wearing Militant Tendency badges," he said.

Mrs Thatcher speaking at Banbury, Oxfordshire denounced the violence as "An attempt to substitute the rule of the mob for the rule of law," She said that the majority of people wanted to see the law upheld.

Thursday May 31st, as the reconvened coal talks went ahead at a secret location in Yorkshire there was further confrontation at Orgreave. The police made another ten arrests outside the coke works, but the talks were calm and showed signs of making some progress. This was in sharp contrast to the previous meeting, on this occasion Ian MacGregor was not present at the negotiating table. The meeting ended with both sides agreeing to hold further talks. Peter Heathfield said he was "optimistic" but adding that there was "still a long way to go."

The week ended as it had began with violent clashes outside Orgreave. Seven police officers and two pickets were taken to Rotherham District Hospital. One picket sustained a fractured skull. Two pickets had to receive mouth to mouth resuscitation from police officers. As lorries left the plant, the pickets estimated to be three thousand, five hundred strong, surged forward and according to Assistant Chief Constable Tony Clement "Six officers were given a good hiding," when they became isolated from their colleagues who numbered two thousand, two hundred.

Nobody who had seen the violence at Orgreave on their television screens each night could fail to be disturbed, it was obviously much more disturbing even terrifying if you were present. There was no doubt that the violence was attributable to both parties. A lot of the injuries sustained by the pickets occurred as they were trying to remove themselves from charging police horses and so were in fact on the retreat. The pitched battles were fought in blazing sunshine and the miners were dressed accordingly i.e. T-shirts, jeans and plimsolls etc. These were people who had travelled to the coke works to take part in orthodox industrial action and who had become embroiled in something else. The police, who took action of the "last resort," were certainly 'expecting' the worst.

Week 13 - Flashpoint – Westminster

Attention was diverted from the picket lines and the coalfields as Parliament become the main focus of the dispute. Confidential documents leaked to 'The Daily Mirror' newspaper revealed Mrs Thatcher had been personally involved in the coal strike despite her consistent denial and even downright refusal to get involved. An inquiry into the leak was ordered by Downing Street, confirming the truth of government involvement. The timing of unsuccessful talks to try and resolve the coal dispute and the successful negotiated settlement in the Rail pay talks on the same day added more significance to the 'Daily Mirror's' revelations. The opposition parties accused the Prime Minister of seriously misleading parliament. She had told Neil Kinnock on April 26th "The government leave the national coal board to get on with the management of the industry within the objectives that it has been given and within the financial arrangements that have been made." On May 3rd she told him, "The government set the external finance limits and then, broadly speaking they leave management to get on with the job. That is what they are doing in the coal industry."

Mr Kinnock claimed "The plain proven fact is that she has intervened, the Prime Minister has not been honest. She has acted cynically in order to try to make political capital out of the dispute." The leader of the Liberal Party, David Steel said that Mrs Thatcher had personally misled Parliament. The row continued on the floor of the House of Commons when the Shadow Transport Spokesman John Prescott demanded an emergency debate saying that the Daily Mirror leak "Clearly exposed the government's strategy of instructing settlements in the Rail industry and other public sector industries in order to prevent further industrial disputes, while it continues it's vendetta against the miners and their families."

The Speaker would not allow an emergency debate. Dennis Skinner MP said "In view of the revelations today, in which it has been made abundantly clear in the Daily Mirror that the Prime Minister has constantly misled the House and treated it with gross contempt by saying there has been no intervention in the miners' strike. I would like to ask you Mr Speaker what steps you are going to take to ensure that the Prime Minister comes to the despatch box today to explain why it is that she is saying one thing in the House and another thing in No 10 – talking to officers of the coal board and British Rail. And if she is not prepared to come are you prepared to refer this to a proper parliamentary committee to see that the Prime Minister is brought to book for this gross contempt." The Speaker said he was not responsible for leaks in newspapers and that he was unable to make the Prime Minister come to the House.

Thursday June 7th, the Palace of Westminster again dominated the news, this time as violence came to it's gates. Miners were in the capital for a mass lobby of Parliament and a rally outside the Greater London Council's HQ County Hall. Arthur Scargill was joined on the platform by Dennis Skinner, Ken Livingstone the leader of the GLC and Mrs Betty Heathfield the wife of the NUM General Secretary, the crowd was estimated to be ten thousand strong.

The demonstration moved across Westminster Bridge chanting "Maggie Out" and singing one of the strike anthems "Here We Go." The ill-feeling between miner and police which had been simmering throughout the strike and which had been brought to the boil with the events at Orgreave, suddenly flared into violence without warning outside the St Stephen's entrance and continued, sporadically for over an hour spilling across Parliament Square. Shouts of 'Sieg Heil' were directed at the police, some of whom were mounted, as fighting continued in the shadow of Churchill's statue, adding a couple of ironic touches to the event. There were more that one hundred arrests, among those arrested was Dave Nellist the Labour MP for Coventry North East. Nellist spent two and a half hours in a cell at Kennington Police Station but was released without being charged.

Inside the House of Commons Stan Orme opened the debate by saying that Mrs Thatcher should have been present to answer the Daily Mirror's disclosure, he accused the Government of seeking a political victory instead of a negotiated settlement.

Peter Walker for the government, refused to answer allegations about the Prime Minister's involvement, but he claimed that government involvement had meant doubling investment in the coal industry, better wages for miners and no compulsory redundancy. Mr Orme moved a Labour motion which condemned the government for it's "Mishandling of the dispute in a way which caused severe hardship to miners and their families." He called for the government to convene a tripartite meeting to discuss 'The Plan for Coal'. An amendment from the government was tabled confirming that the coal industry's future was dependent on it's competitiveness with other fuels. A Liberal-SDP alliance amendment which criticised all parties concerned in the strike was not put to the vote.

Mr Orme said that if investment had been made to so-called uneconomic pits they would not be uneconomic, jeered by Tory MPs he retorted "When you laugh you are laughing at people losing their jobs." He denounced the government for deeming strikers to receive £15 a week in strike pay as "One of the government's most vicious moves against working people. Other benefits have been denied in an attempt to starve the miners back to work." Walker challenged Orme to say that he would not close any pit no matter how uneconomic. Dennis Skinner intervened and said that it was estimated that the coal industry was subsidised by

£135 per miner per week, but if it were subsidised at the same rate as farmers "Like Mr Walker and some of his friends," there would be no such thing as an uneconomic pit. He added that if the miners received the equivalent of the £400,000 per job on offer to Nissan the miners would be living in the lap of luxury. One miner was ejected from the public gallery for applauding Mr Skinner.

Mr Walker then repeated his earlier statements referring to higher investment, decent wages and no compulsory redundancies. The former leader of the opposition, Michael Foot MP for Blaenau Gwent accused ministers of a conspiracy between the government and the NCB, "Appointing MacGregor to the job was part of that conspiracy," he said. Then turning to the leak in the Daily Mirror he told the energy secretary "It is significant that in the whole of your speech you did not refer to the developments of the last few days. It is a disgrace that the Prime Minister has not come down to the House to make a statement on the matter. On a number of occasions she has said that there has been no intervention in the dispute, that there will be none. Now we have clear indications that is not the case and that the Prime Minister intervened."

Mr Foot, amid Tory jeers spoke of the bitterness created in the mining communities, "That bitterness will be increased when they read how the Prime Minister has lied to this House and the Country," he added. Mr Foot was stopped on a point of order by Andrew Stewart the Conservative MP for Sherwood who praised the working miners and said "We will see the coal produced by men who put their country and their families before political philosophy."

Away from Westminster the confrontation at Orgreave seemed to be becoming a daily ritual with pickets and police vying for tactical supremacy. The worst violence of the week occurred on Wednesday June 6th when there were twenty three arrests. Twelve people were injured including eight policemen. Arthur Scargill was present and it was inferred that his presence on the picket line provoked the violent scenes in which the police lines were allegedly pelted with ball-bearings and paint stripper.

In Nottinghamshire police turned away one thousand flying pickets who were descending on working pits. There were, however, arrests outside Warsop and Welbeck collieries.

A new development saw a kind of luddism creeping into the dispute, this would become a regular feature of the strike and showed signs of both frustration and indeed desperation among some of the strikers. Over £5,000 worth of damage was inflicted on seven pit top conveyor belts at Silverdale colliery, Staffordshire.

Week 14 - Other Forces At Work

Another serious and complicating factor, that of the deterioration of pits due to the prolonged stoppage, was introduced into the dispute by the NCB. James Cowan had raised the matter during the talks with the NUM saying that as many as a quarter of the board's collieries could be affected or even lost should lengthy stoppages take the dispute into the Autumn. Mr Cowan's warning was followed by an announcement from Mr Albert Wheeler, head of the NCB's Scottish Area, that four of Scotland's pits faced closure because of damage caused by the strike. The face at Comrie colliery in West Fife was said to be in a state of serious deterioration. Castlehill colliery in West Fife was suffering from rapidly deteriorating roadways and it's face was in need of urgent attention. Barony colliery in Ayrshire was subject to a squeezing effect with roof and floor coming together. Seafield's main face was said to be suffering from severe structural deterioration. Even if an element of bluff was intended by the board it was obviously a development that must be taken very seriously by both board and union.

A joint branch meeting of ASLEF and NUR at Shirebrook, Derbyshire voted to block all movement of coal from Nottinghamshire for a fortnight.

Tuesday June 12th, the Wales TUC went ahead with it's day of action, against the wishes of Len Murray. An estimated ten thousand marchers took part in a rally at Cardiff which was addressed by David Jenkins General Secretary of the Wales TUC, Rodney Bickerstaff General Secretary of NUPE, Emlyn Williams and Tony Benn. Mr Benn informed the rally "If the Wales TUC had waited for permission from the General Council we would not be having this demonstration today." Welsh miners were joined on the march by a group of striking Leicestershire miners and by a Sheffield Women's Support Group. Elsewhere in the Principality bus services, docks, hospitals, factories and government offices faced disruption.

Margaret Thatcher and Neil Kinnock clashed bitterly in the Commons. Mr Kinnock accused the Prime Minister of deceit saying "The evidence of your deceit is also proven and the way you are involved when you claim not to be involved, and are involved for all the wrong reasons." Mrs Thatcher said that government involvement had been restricted to providing investment cash and funds for redundancy payments. "If that is intervention I have intervened. But to No10 and beer and sandwiches, no, never." The SDP leader, Dr David Owen called for the civil law to be invoked to deal with secondary picketing. The Prime Minister said the government would not over-ride any invocation of the civil law.

On the eve of the third round of coal talks a row developed between Scargill and MacGregor. MacGregor had warned in an interview with the 'Times' newspaper that the longer the dispute lasted "The less certain we are going to be able to go through with our stated objective of carrying out the reduction in capacity with the minimum or possible zero mandatory redundancies." This contradicted the board's objective to rule out compulsory redundancy. Scargill responded on BBC radio by saying "I would not trust Mr MacGregor if he told me the time of day." Surprise, annoyance and frustration was caused by this row breaking out at such a delicate time.

Wednesday June 13th, a Rotherham hotel was the venue for the third round of coal talks. Set against the background of animosity created by the untimely remarks of the NCB chairman, it caused little surprise when the talks broke down after one and a half hours. Both sides were sticking to their guns and the divide was as great as when the strike began.

Next day the rift widened with Ian MacGregor threatening to call a national ballot over the head of the union and Arthur Scargill responded by saying that such a ballot "Smacked of the sinister approach of Americanism." Mick McGahey claimed "Other forces were at work," a clear reference that he believed the government had, had it's way in the outcome of the talks.

Roy Hattersley, deputising for Neil Kinnock who was absent campaigning in the European elections, challenged the Prime Minister in the Commons during question time. "Following the breakdown of the pit peace talks, do you intend to continue with the pretence that you have been sitting on the sidelines watching the damage continue or will you encourage an honourable negotiated settlement that would clearly be in the national interest?" Mrs Thatcher replied "No I will not have a meeting at No 10 and call both sides together in any way. This strike was always unnecessary. It has gone on too long. I hope those people on strike will think carefully about their positions and return to work."

An agreement between the South Wales NUM and the steel unions about the supply of coal to Llanwern was scuppered by Arthur Scargill who said the matter must be negotiated nationally.

Bob Clay MP (Labour - Sunderland North) was convicted of obstructing a police officer by Bishop Auckland magistrates, he was fined £50 and ordered to pay £50 costs.

There were twenty eight arrests at Bickershaw colliery, Lancashire, when one thousand miners, confronted by four hundred police attempted to prevent working miners from clocking on. In Nottinghamshire there were twenty arrests outside Harworth colliery. Police were pelted with eggs and running fights broke out, the picket line was estimated to be one thousand, five hundred strong.

The weekend saw rioting on the streets of Maltby, South Yorkshire – a village just a few miles from Orgreave. Friday June 15th, 200 young people gathered outside the police station and hurled missiles at the police. Reinforcements were called and there were sixteen arrests. There was a repeat of the incident on Saturday, this time the police were prepared and they made twenty nine arrests. Mr Peter Wright the Chief Constable of South Yorkshire said that tension caused by the strike could have been a contributory factor.

On Friday June 15th Mr Joe Green aged fifty five of Knottingley and employed underground at Kellingley colliery North Yorkshire was killed when he was hit by a lorry while peacefully picketing outside Ferrybridge Power station West Yorkshire.

Week 15 - "Unlawful Assembly"

In the next attempt of the many attempts by the NCB to break the strike, Ian MacGregor announced his intention to send a personal plea to every member of the NUM hoping to stimulate a drift back to work. This move was seen to supercede his original intention of balloting the union. It was believed that some senior coal board officials and even some cabinet ministers feared that such a move could prove to be counter-productive and may alienate moderates. The letter was intended to clear up doubts which miners may have about the board's plans. It was "Part of MacGregor's strategy to by-pass the trade union organisation," said Peter Heathfield and he claimed it was "Doomed to failure."

> This is a strike which should never have happened. It is based on very serious misrepresentation and distortion of the facts. At great financial cost miners have supported the strike for fourteen weeks because your leaders have told you this .....
>
> That the Coal Board is out to butcher the coal industry.
> That we plan to do away with 70,000 jobs.
> That we plan to close down around 86 pits, leaving only 100 working collieries.
>
> IF THESE THINGS WERE TRUE I WOULD NOT BLAME MINERS FOR GETTING ANGRY OR FOR BEING DEEPLY WORRIED. BUT THESE THINGS ARE ABSOLUTELY UNTRUE. I STATE THAT CATEGORICALLY AND SOLEMNLY. YOU HAVE BEEN DELIBERATELY MISLED.

Monday June 18th, unprecedented scenes of violence were seen outside the Orgreave coke works, during ten hours of violent clashes which began at 3 am the police made ninety three arrests. Fifty one pickets sustained injuries compared with twenty eight police who were also hurt. Among those injured was Arthur Scargill who was detained overnight at Rotherham infirmary suffering from head, leg and arm injuries. Police wore riot gear and mounted charges were made. Truncheons were used on pickets by police snatch squads. Pickets were said to have thrown missiles of every description, cars were burned and police claimed that two petrol bombs had been thrown. Police cheered as one picket, bleeding profusely from a head wound, was helped to a waiting ambulance.

There were conflicting accounts of how Scargill received his injuries, he himself claimed he had been hit with a riot shield, when a TV reporter tried to interview the NUM President who was visibly shaken he clearly indicated the police were to blame. A miner claimed Mr Scargill was hurt during a police charge. 'Fortunately' the police eye witness was one Anthony Clement who said he saw Mr Scargill slip near some chain link fencing and fall backwards against what the Ass't Chief Constable thought was a railway sleeper. Clement who was heading the police operation numbering some three thousand, four hundred officers said later that it was a miracle that no-one was killed.

There were also twenty one arrests outside Shirebrook colliery, North Derbyshire as pickets attempted to prevent a return to work, but the police were successful in escorting the blacklegs into the pit.

In the House of Commons the attorney General Sir Michael Havers said the miners at Orgreave were not pickets, but demonstrators and rioters in many cases. Later in the commons Tony Benn called for a fresh Commons debate on the seriousness of "Pitched battles involving hundreds of people and amounting in some cases to almost civil war proportions." He said the government was "In effect running an emergency regime" and that emergency powers had to be debated and approved by the House. The Speaker said the issue was open to be raised by normal procedure. Picket line violence was condemned by both the Prime Minister, and the Leader of the Opposition.

Next day after being discharged from hospital, Arthur Scargill said he felt a bit groggy and he accused the police of showing blind hatred to the miners. There were angry scenes in the House of Commons. Mrs Thatcher condemned what she called "Mob Rule" and repeatedly challenged Neil Kinnock to condemn the violence (one began to wonder how many times he was expected to do this, how long the Conservatives would lay the bait and how many times the bait would be accepted.) However, Kinnock replied "I have repeatedly condemned without reservation the use of violence by any and all parties in industrial dispute." After the debate Eldon Griffiths the Conservative MP for Bury St Edmunds and the parliamentary spokesman for the Police Federation, tabled a Commons motion censuring "Bogus condemnations of violence on picket lines."

It was also a week which witnessed an attempt to break the strike in Kent which led to a three day sit-in by six miners at Betteshanger colliery, thus preventing safety work being carried out at the pit. The men stayed underground, while forty others staged a sit-in at a pithead office despite a possession order being obtained by the coal board. They only agreed to call off their protest after an assurance from two miners that there would be no attempt to return to work.

Friday June 22nd, Arthur Scargill and Jack Taylor attended the funeral in Pontefract of Mr Joe Green. The mourners were led by a lone piper who played "The Flowers of the Forest."

Saturday June 23rd, Margaret Thatcher addressed the Welsh Conservative Conference at Porthcawl, Mid-Glamorgan, she described mass picketing as "Unlawful Assembly." Outside she was barracked by a demonstration organised by Womens' Support Groups and a protest by farmers demonstrating against EEC milk quotas. An egg was thrown by the farmers' action group, it scored a direct hit.

Week 16 - The Convoy

The temperature of the coal strike was raised again when in retaliation to the BSC moving coal by road the NUR agreed to stop the delivery of iron ore to Llanwern. This action was taken after failure by the NUM to get the steel unions to agree reduced production levels at the BSC's five integrated plants i.e. Ravenscraig, Redcar, Scunthorpe, Port Talbot and Llanwern. Union leaders at Llanwern announced they would use coal and iron ore from any source to ensure the survival of their plant. Despite teething troubles during the first few days, the NUM picket lines were receiving support from the rail unions and British Rail were sending their crews home without pay.

Then the impossible happened when the BSC decided to move the iron ore, essential to production, by road. Llanwern required 50,000 tonnes of iron ore each week and to transport this volume by road necessitated an around the clock operation. But on Friday June 29th, pickets were caught napping as over a hundred lorries with police protection carried ore at high speed between Port Talbot and Llanwern. Another convoy of some fifty lorries were making the same run carrying coal. Two lorries had their windscreens smashed at Port Talbot.

Mr Phillip Weeks, the NCB Director for South Wales said that nine of the Area's pits depended on Llanwern steelworks as it was one of the coal board's best customers and therefore it was in the miners' interests to supply the plant with Welsh coal. During the steel strike in 1980 the NCB had urged the NUM not to support the strikers as other markets could easily be found for Welsh coal.

It is interesting to note that had the steel unions been able to reach an agreement with the NUM over steel production levels, the steelworks' quarterly production bonus would have been adversely affected. This would have highlighted the bonus scheme, which had been negotiated in lieu of a wage increase, to be an inadequate compensation. The steelworks would also then realise, once the bonus scheme had been stripped away, that they had not received a real wage increase since the one which had settled their own dispute four years earlier. This leads to the question of how the steel unions would pursue a future wage demand successfully; a strike by these unions alone seems the unlikely answer. Margaret Thatcher's age of new realism for the trade unions relied on the theory that if you do not have the muscle to win a major dispute first time round, you will not have the inclination for a re-match. The 1980 strike had knocked the stuffing out of the steelworkers or to put it another way, most of the stuffing had been made redundant in 1981.

Away from the convoy and its implications week sixteen had seen fifty arrests outside Bilston Glen colliery near Edinburgh when about five hundred strikers failed to prevent thirty eight miners reporting for work.

Week 17 - "Constructive Discussions"

Mr MacGregor had one of his more inconsistent weeks. The week began with an attack by the NCB chairman on picket line violence, when in a BBC radio interview he accused the NUM of orchestrating the confrontation. The coal board chairman also revealed that he had received letters from "unwilling strikers" who said that they feared reprisals if they returned to work.

The Home Secretary Leon Brittan criticised Mr Scargill for failing to condemn the intimidation of working miners. Scargill condemned the intimidation of striking miners in Nottinghamshire, when he said "The fact that we have police officers, both in uniform and plain clothes, knocking on doors in the middle of the night, to see if there are miners from other parts of the British coalfield in attendance, is an indication of how far down the slippery slope we have come."

The NUM President once again met with representatives of the fourteen steel unions, but failed to get support for the production cuts that he was seeking.

The BSC increased its convoy from Port Talbot to Llanwern to one hundred and seven lorries making three runs a day. The TGWU Regional Secretary Mr George Wright accused South Wales police of "Assisting hauliers to operate illegally in a strike breaking situation," claiming that some of the lorries being used were unlicensed. Wright said disciplinary action would be taken against companies and drivers involved in the convoy. Later fourteen drivers belonging to Hazell Transport of Newport and George Road Transport of the Forest of Dean, Gloucestershire, were excluded from the union.

Arthur Scargill announced that the NUM had been contacted by the NCB and that new talks would take place. Mr MacGregor said "We shall be endeavouring to have constructive discussions," saying that the talks were a new opportunity to settle the dispute. Then on the eve of the new talks Ian MacGregor said he doubted whether he could change his mind on pit closures but, he denied that a personality clash existed between himself and Mr Scargill.

The talks took place in a London Hotel and they were to run into the next week. There was a degree of optimism that progress was being made as on Thursday 5th and Friday 6th July the talks lasted a total of 14 ½ hours. Arthur Scargill took time off to tell a ten thousand strong rally at Birmingham, "We are going to win." So it had been a week of verbal jousting by the NUM President and the NCB Chairman, but the confrontation also continued elsewhere. In South Wales, miners from St John's colliery, Maesteg formed their own convoy of cars and tried to disrupt the progress of the lorry convoy on the M4. Police stopped the cars but no arrests were made.

In a two pronged attack, pickets took police by surprise at Llanwern and Port

Talbot, three lorries had windows smashed by a barrage of missiles. In all, there were twenty eight arrests. The South Wales NUM research officer Dr Kim Howells said "This was a token stepping up to check police response. We may now bring many more men in."

The NCB stepped up its campaign for a return to work by deciding to lay on transport for any miner wishing to return.

Week 18 - The First Dock Strike

During this week some of the most complicated developments so far took place. The coal talks which had been in session since the previous week were adjourned in limbo for nine days. The adjournment came at a delicate stage in the negotiations. The NCB wanted to define as exhausted any pit with "No further mineable reserves that are workable or which can be beneficially developed." The union objected to the word beneficial being included. The NUM wanted the future of the five pits originally named for closure guaranteed. The NCB had agreed that the pits should be "subject to further consideration." Ian MacGregor commented later "We are not giving in to the miners. We are laying down a programme which makes the future of the business feasible. It shows we are at least pragmatic, which is more that can be said for the other side." The reason for the adjournment of talks was to accommodate a special NUM conference at Sheffield.

The NUM special conference was the subject of a special evening hearing in the High Court. The Vice-Chancellor Sir Robert Megarry ruled that the conference should not discuss or vote on a proposed rule change for disciplining working miners. The application for the injunction came from working Notts miners, aggrieved that they had not had an opportunity to mandate their national executive members because their area council meeting had been picketed out. Following a meeting of the NUM national executive Mr Scargill said "We are an independent, free and democratic trade union operating on the basis of our rules and constitution. Our conference tomorrow will go ahead in the normal way." As stated by Arthur Scargill the conference went ahead on Wednesday July 11th and passed a new disciplinary code on a card vote. The change to rule 51 was carried by 166,000 votes to 62,000. The new rule enabled the union to set up a national disciplinary committee and a national appeals committee, both to be re-elected every three years. The seven member disciplinary committee would be chaired by Mick McGahey and the nine man appeals committee by Arthur Scargill. Individual, branch, area and national discipline would be catered for by the new procedure. The conference also passed a unanimous resolution against the pit closure programme for the NUM leaders to take into adjourned talks with the coal board on their resumption.

From midnight on Monday July 9th, the TGWU ordered a national docks strike. The strike was called in protest at the BSC use of non-dockers to unload ore 'blacked' in support of the miners' strike at Immingham docks, Humberside. The lightning strike sparked by the ore which was for use at Scunthorpe steel works, hid the main issue which was seen by the union as a threat to the National

Dock Labour Scheme, under which, since 1947, only registered dockers have been allowed to work in ports covered by the scheme.

All the big ports covered by the scheme responded to the strike call. At London, Tilbury, Liverpool, Southampton, Manchester, Hull, Glasgow, Aberdeen, Bristol, Cardiff and at Swansea work came to a standstill as the employers and union met in London to attempt to find a solution. In the non scheme ports the response was patchy, with ferry ports, notably Dover, continuing to work, however, Felixstowe came out as the first talks collapsed. Talks resumed later in the week but again broke down with the TGWU threatening to step up action to hit holidaymakers.

The TGWU National Docks Secretary John Connolly said "We don't want to impose hardship, but because we cannot have an agreement on selective action we have to recommend a total stoppage." The strike was welcomed by miners' leaders and the NUR and the NUS pledged their support.

Other than these major developments week eighteen saw fresh confrontation in Yorkshire. At Rossington colliery near Doncaster, thirteen coal board officials had to be rescued by police after being besieged by about three hundred pickets for eleven hours. It was decided to abandon the colliery. Meanwhile at the nearby village of Hemsworth the police station was stoned. A similar incident occurred at Kinsley open-cast mine near Barnsley when seven officials and two security men had to barricade themselves in as men went on the rampage causing an estimated £100,000 worth of damage. Margaret Thatcher called the Rossington incident "Industrial Anarchy."

The week ended with the Durham miners' gala and Arthur Scargill was joined on the platform by Neil Kinnock, the Labour Party leader traditionally addresses the Durham Gala. Attended by fifteen thousand people, Kinnock told the 101st Durham Gala "Coal is vital to recovery, to prosperity, and to the whole community and that's why we can't allow this industry to be shrivelled up by Margaret Thatcher. That's why we can't allow Margaret Thatcher and her government to let this industry and the coal communities rot. That's why we can't permit Thatcher to have a further victory in her war against the British people. This is a fight in the mining communities for survival."

Week 19 - The End Of The First Dock Strike

The Secretary of State for Wales Nicholas Edwards told MPs during Welsh Question Time that the appearance of Labour Leader Neil Kinnock at the Durham miners' Gala gave backing to a political strike, he added "I find it profoundly shocking that the leader of a major political party should associate himself with violence and intimidation and a strike which can only do grave damage to jobs and unemployment levels." Michael Foot defended his successor who was not present, saying "What the leader of the Opposition wants, what every sensible person in the country wants is to see this dispute brought to an end under the proper procedures which were agreed under the 'plan for coal'.

On the eve of the resumption of the coal talks, hopes of a settlement waned following statements by both the union and the board. Scargill speaking after a meeting with the TGWU said the NCB had "Promised to withdraw the pit closure programme announced on March 16th, they have promised to reach an agreement along the lines of our original suggestion for what is deemed exhausted. Yet they will not put these promises in writing. It does suggest that Mrs Thatcher's hands are on the negotiating table." Mr Scargill accused the government of conducting a vendetta against the NUM, he asked "Are we talking about defeating a trade union leader and the NUM or are we talking about solving a damaging and difficult dispute caused by the NCB violating a signed agreement?"

Ian MacGregor said he had made the board's final offer "The NCB have for many years and without major conflict reached agreement with the NUM on closing pits for other reasons apart from exhaustion and safety. These reasons have varied from poor geological conditions to low quality coal, but have always amounted to the fact that the cost of coal from those pits has become too high to justify continuing to mine them."

The Coal Board Chairman also said that the overtime ban that the NUM had imposed against the board's 5.2% pay offer would have to be lifted and that strikers would have to learn to work with fellow miners who had ignored the strike call in order to reach a settlement. Arthur Scargill had already stated that strikers would not work with scabs.

Monday July 16th, saw forty two arrests in a renewed confrontation at Port Talbot. Two policemen and one picket required hospital treatment. About four hundred pickets attempted to stop the lorry convoy leaving the steelworks bound for Llanwern, windscreens were smashed as two hundred police struggled to keep control. A police spokesman said the miners had broken the agreement to shorten the Port Talbot picket line.

Tuesday July 17th, Down's wharf, a private wharf at Newport, Gwent, was the scene of twenty four arrests including one woman, as one hundred pickets tried to prevent lorries carrying fuel imported from Germany to Llanwern. Three of those arrested were striking dockers.

Wednesday July 18th, the coal talks took place in London against the pessimistic scene which the leaders had set, the talks collapsed amid some acrimony on Thursday July 19th.

At the House of Commons Margaret Thatcher addressing the Monday Club, the committee of Conservative backbench MPs, declared "We had to fight the enemy without in the Falklands. We always have to be aware of the enemy within, which is much more difficult to fight and more dangerous to liberty." The Prime Minister, always looking for an enemy to fight was now comparing the NUM with the Argentinian Junta. The government laid the blame with Mr Scargill for the breakdown in negotiations. Peter Walker led the offensive and he was joined by Tom King and Norman Tebbitt, the Energy Secretary said "It can only be the desire to impose on Britain the type of socialist state that the British electorate constantly rejects that motivates Mr Scargill to continue to do so much damage to his industry, an industry that is now losing markets and customers." The board's unwillingness to delete the phrase "beneficially developed" relating to mineable reserves of coal which had raised union objections the previous week, was the cause of the breakdown of talks.

The South Wales Area NUM leadership Emlyn Williams, Vice-President Terry Thomas and the General Secretary George Rees were served with High Court writs over the picketing of Port Talbot steelworks. The action against the three top area officials was taken for non-compliance with an injunction which had been granted in April to Richard Read Transport and George T Read Transport both of the Forest of Dean, Gloucestershire, to stop the NUM interfering with their lorries which were forming part of the convoy. The three NUM leaders said they would not attend the hearing and would not be represented in court. The union was also in trouble nationally when Sir Robert Megarry declared the use of the new disciplinary code illegal. The orders were granted to seventeen working members of the Notts NUM, the NUM were not represented in High Court.

The Transport Secretary Nicholas Ridley told the commons that the Dock Strike, which had now been extended to Dover freight traffic, was being continued under false pretences in support of the miners. In a statement to a noisy House Mr Ridley said the Immingham dispute had been resolved and that the government had no intention to abolish the Dock Labour Scheme. Talks in the dispute were arranged by the arbitration service ACAS and they were successfully concluded at midnight on Saturday 21st. The talks which lasted a total of sixteen hours ended the strike when it was agreed by the National Association of Port Employers that employers would use non-registered labour only after applying to their local Dock Labour Board.

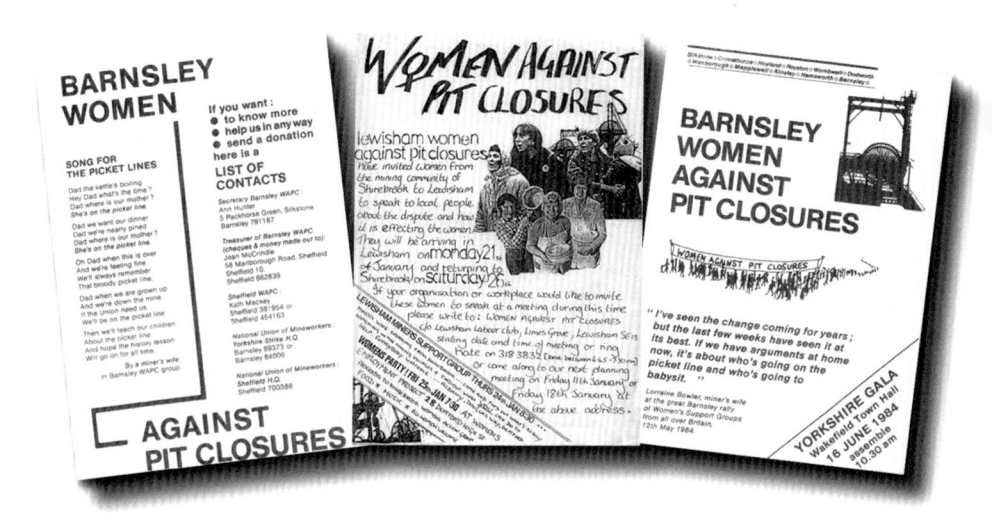

Week 20 - The Silver Birch

Tuesday July 24th, South Wales pickets launched a two-pronged action, aimed at stopping the convoys between Port Talbot and Llanwern. The grass verges adjacent to the M4 motorway were set on fire sending a smokescreen across the road. The convoy was delayed from leaving the Margam gate of Port Talbot steelworks for well over an hour. The five hundred strong picket line had been reinforced by around two hundred women from Womens' Support Groups throughout South Wales and a group of women about twenty strong from the Greenham Common Peace Camp who were showing the NUM reciprocal support. The three hundred police made twenty nine arrests including seven women. One policeman was slightly injured. The demonstration had been peaceful but it erupted soon after the initial arrests for obstructing the highway by sitting on the road. As the lorries left the steelworks pickets hurled stones and five windscreens were broken. Meanwhile at Llanwern two hundred pickets were outflanked by police who re-directed the convoy to a different gate at the plant. There were six arrests.

Elsewhere there were thirty three arrests outside Bilston Glen colliery near Edinburgh and a blockade of the Humber Bridge by some five hundred miners in about one hundred cars led to twenty six arrests. The day of confrontation was the union's reply to a national back to work campaign being orchestrated by working miners in Nottinghamshire. Any trickle back to work in striking areas would force the NUM to fight a rearguard action. The man supposedly leading the strike-breaking campaign was Nottinghamshire miner Mr Chris Butcher, aged 33, employed as a blacksmith at Bevercotes colliery, who for reasons best know to himself was operating under the nickname of "The Silver Birch."

Friday July 27th, the NUM President made his first appearance in the South Wales coalfield since the strike began. Organised by the Abertillery Womens' Support Group, Arthur Scargill addressed a crowd of three thousand marchers in the picturesque surroundings of Abertillery Park the home of Abertillery Rugby Football Club. He told the rally that steelworkers and lorry drivers should show solidarity with the strikers, the miners' leader said "When workers are involved in strike action you do not cross picket lines." Scargill was sharing the platform with the South Wales Area Vice-President Terry Thomas who mocked the back-to-work campaign and he reaffirmed that the area officials would not comply with anti-trade union laws. Other speakers included the Leader of the Opposition's wife Mrs Glenys Kinnock, Ms Jo Richardson MP, the local Member of Parliament Michael Foot, Llew Smith the recently elected MEP for South East Wales and Councillor Brian Scully the Leader of Blaenau Gwent Borough Council.

Week 21 - Seizure Of South Wales Assets

A fine of £50,000 was imposed on the South Wales NUM by Mr Justice Park in the High Court, for contempt of court, the union were given forty eight hours to pay, or have their entire assets estimated at £3,000,000 sequestrated. The penalty was imposed by the judge under the employment Acts of 1980 and 1982, the only other time that sequestration (confiscation of assets) had been enforced was against the National Graphical Association for non-payment of a fine incurred in a dispute with newspaper owner Mr Eddie Shah. Following a meeting of the South Wales Area Executive at Pontypridd, Mid-Glamorgan, it was decided to run the risk of sequestration by not paying the fine. A city firm of Chartered Accountants, Price Waterhouse, were appointed by the court to act as sequestrators. The response by Arthur Scargill was "It has not yet penetrated the minds of this government or the judiciary that you cannot sequestrate an idea, nor imprison a belief. The High Court decision is yet another blatant example of interference in the affairs of an independent trade union fighting for the right to work. I call on the British trade union movement to now honour the undertakings made at the TUC special conference in Wembley and give total physical support to the NUM, currently under attack from the government's anti-trade union legislation."

In defiance the union barricaded themselves into their offices at Crumlin and Swansea and also at their Pontypridd headquarters. A rally of support was held at Pontypridd and Emlyn Williams told the crowd "We'll fight, we'll win or we'll die in the attempt."

Within days the South Wales NUM assets had been frozen. The Co-operative Bank issued a statement in which it said it would - act in accordance with the sequestrator's instructions. Food and relief funds were put in jeopardy and Dr Kim Howells; South Wales NUM research officer said "The government is going for the most vulnerable target, hitting miners' families where it hurts most – in the belly."

Tuesday July 31st, during stormy scenes in the House of Commons at Prime Minister's question time, Martin Flannery, the Labour MP for Sheffield Hillsborough was 'named' by the Speaker and suspended from the House for five days after claiming that "Lame Tory judges" were being used against the miners. Later in the 'censure' debate called for by the opposition to criticise the government's handling of the dispute, Mrs Thatcher clashed with Mr Kinnock describing his polices as "appeasement" and then she turned her attention on Tony Benn claiming he had sanctioned the closure of uneconomic pits when he was Labour's Energy Secretary.

There was further depressing news when a report written by the NCB's head of mining Mr Ronald Price stated that as many as sixty coalfaces were at risk due to geological problems caused by the strike.

The Chancellor of the Exchequer Nigel Lawson said the cost of the coal strike was a "Worthwhile investment for the good of the nation." This clearly indicated the government's intention of a fight to the finish, no matter how much money that course of action may eventually cost.

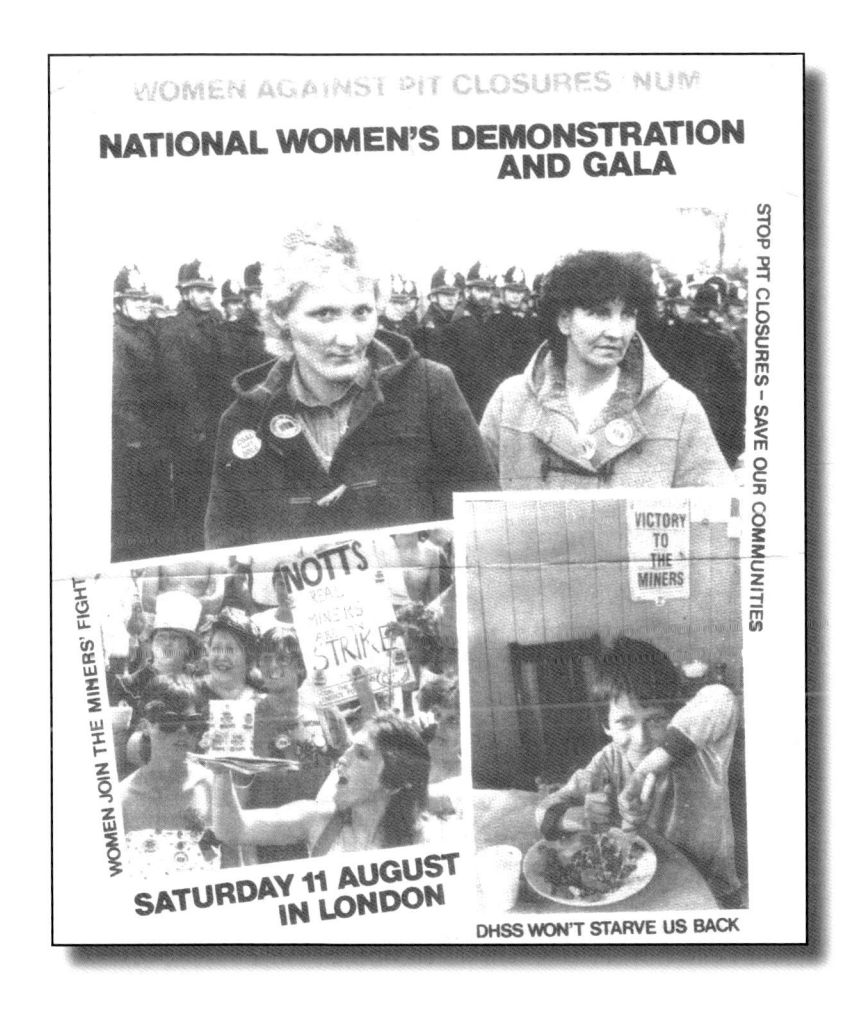

Week 22 - Flashpoint – Harworth

The South Wales area NUM were taken totally by surprise when two of their number returned to work. Monty Morgan was the first to return, at Garw colliery. He reported to the pit manager and went to the lamp room, but the withdrawal of a safety cover by the union prevented him going underground. After reporting for work twice he was persuaded to rejoin the strike – two days later he again reported for work. This time he was confronted by hundreds of pickets, Mr Morgan had to be transported home by police when a bus driver who had been ordered to take him home refused to cross the picket line, the pit was picketed by virtually the whole village. By the weekend, ostracised by the community called "scab" and "English bastard" (he came originally from Leamington Spa) Morgan agreed again to abandon his return to work. During one demonstration outside the colliery the police made eleven arrests.

Meanwhile at Cwm colliery near Beddau, Tommy Hughes became the second South Wales miner to breach the strike. But by the end of the day he had rejoined the strike and he had even volunteered for picket duty, following a threat from the NUM to withdraw safety cover.

Wednesday August 8th, confrontation returned to the Nottinghamshire coal field when fifty nine arrests were made outside Harworth colliery in the north of the county, just south of the Yorkshire border. Working miners were pelted with missiles and then the pickets estimated at eight hundred retreated into the village streets. Mounted police were deployed against the pickets, missiles were thrown at police vehicles and coal lorries. The day before had witnessed a trail of destruction. Canteen windows had been broken at Harworth colliery and cars belonging to working miners were damaged. Another Nottinghamshire pit, Silverhill colliery had also been a target and the NCB offices at Doncaster was also attacked.

There was some light relief in South Wales, when Jazz singer George Melly threw his weight behind the Gwent and Rhymney Valley Food Fund by performing three benefit concerts at Newbridge, Caerphilly and Llanhilleth.

The week ended with various back-to-work campaigns being mooted in the coalfields while on Saturday August 11th, London was the scene of a womens' Support March and Rally.

Thousands of miners' wives and supporters from all over Britain converged on the capital. Mrs Betty Heathfield and Mrs Ann Scargill went to Buckingham Palace to present a petition aimed at drawing the Queen's attention to the plight of striking miners and their families.

Week 23 - The Spirit Of '39

Arthur Scargill attended a meeting in Cardiff together with Ray Buckton (ASLEF,) Ron Todd (TGWU General Secretary Elect,) George Wright (TGWU,) Sam McCluskie (NUS) and Charles Turnock (NUR.) The meeting had been called to thrash out a common policy to put before the TUC conference. It also planned a joint defence against George Read Transport one of the haulage firms who had instigated the court action which had led to the sequestration of the South Wales NUM funds and who were now threatening the TGWU with similar action because of 'blacking' resulting from the dock strike.

Management and NACODS members were besieged at St John's colliery, Maesteg by about one hundred and fifty pickets for thirty six hours. The siege was an attempt to persuade the St John's NACODS lodge to join the strike as the pit was one which was tipped for closure, the siege ended peacefully. Also in South Wales there were four arrests when about seventy pickets tried to prevent coal lorries entering Aberthaw cement works.

Fifteen miners undertook an occupation at the offices of Price Waterhouse, in Birmingham. The protest, organized in conjunction with Birmingham Trades Council, was against the seizure of benevolent and welfare funds by the accountancy firm.

The week saw the return to work of the first Yorkshire miner. Brian Green returned to work at the Gascoigne Wood coal handling plant near Selby. His return was dismissed by Jack Taylor who said, "He's just 1 in 55,000." Before the week was out another had returned at Gascoigne Wood and according to the NCB seven had now returned in Yorkshire. Peter Heathfield said, "I think it is rather sad that a handful of people have responded to the NCB'S propaganda campaign. I think they will find themselves in a lonely position. We have been monitoring the situation very closely and it conflicts strongly with the NCB's account. It is not even a dribble. It is of no consequence." However, on Friday 17th August, Gascoigne Wood was the scene of violent clashes as three miners reported for work, nine policeman were injured as were four pickets and there were six arrests. An estimated three thousand pickets driven into a ploughed field by a police baton charge responded by throwing mud at the aggressors. The arrival of the three miners was delayed by almost three hours.

In the high court Mr Justice Hutchinson called a halt to the seizure of the South Wales NUM's assets. The judge authorized that the £50,000 fine should be paid from the £707,000 which the sequestrators had already seized and that the costs of the two haulage firms should also be met from the same source.

For the NUM the week ended on Saturday August 18th with a march which re-enacted the Chartist March of 1839. The March converged from the Gwent valleys to a rally at Shaftesbury Park Newport. Emlyn Williams and the Yorkshire NUM General Secretary Owen Briscoe were joined on the platform by Michael Foot, Roy Hughes the Labour MP for Newport East, South East Wales Euro MP Llew Smith and GLC member Neil Davies one of whose forebears had taken part in the 1839 march which had ended in bloody confrontation with the military outside the town's Westgate Hotel.

For the NCB's part the week ended with Ian MacGregor accusing Athur Scargill of trying to intimidate other unions into supporting the miners at the forth coming TUC conference to be held in September. He said, "Scargill has gone out of his way to intimidate his own members now he wants to intimidate other unions. And he wants to steam up the left periphery of the TUC to take part in various embargoes to help the NUM. But he has to depend on the national organisers of these left wing unions because the members won't do it. So he is urging those left wing leaders to de-democratise their unions too, just as he has the NUM." He also inferred that September 3rd would be the date of a national 'back to work drive,' he said a big turn out of pickets at the Trades Union Congress at Brighton would mean that there would be fewer pickets in the coalfields.

SAVE OUR COMMUNITIES – DEMONSTRATE FOR JOBS

We call on working people in all industries, all men and women from our communities, to join with us and demonstrate along part of the historic route of the Chartist march to Newport. Representatives of trade unions from all over Britain and abroad will be there. Make sure you are.

SATURDAY, AUGUST 18th

Demonstrations will be held at the following places: TREDEGAR, BLACKWOOD, CROSSKEYS, RISCA, EBBW VALE, ABERTILLERY, CRUMLIN, NEWBRIDGE, BLAENAVON, PONTYPOOL, CWMBRAN. (All commencing at 9.30 a.m.).

See local posters and press for further details, or 'phone: PONTYPOOL 3387; NEWBRIDGE 244313/243215/244713; BARGOED 834045.

GREAT RALLY, NEWPORT

(Travel, from earlier marches, by coach).

ASSEMBLE: 12 Noon ALLT YR YN. To march via Stow Hill, Westgate Hotel and on to Shaftesbury Park.

SPEAKERS

NEIL DAVIES (Greater London Council)
OWEN BRISCOE (Gen. Sec. Yorkshire NUM)
MICHAEL FOOT, MP
(and other speakers)

Week 24 - Flashpoint - Armthorpe/The Second Dock Strike

Ian Macgregor whilst visiting the site of a proposed new £400 million mine at Ashfordby near Melton Mowbray, Leicestershire, again accused Arthur Scargill and the NUM leadership of orchestrating coalfield violence. He cited the coachloads of pickets being taken to Bilston Glen colliery near Loanhead from Yorkshire and the North-East to reinforce the Scottish pickets "It takes some form of central brain to produce this spontaneous reaction" said the NCB chairman. Referring to the working miners he said "The fact that they are being intimidated out by criminal action orchestrated by Mr Scargill and his friends is some reflection on this country." Arthur Scargill dismissed MacGregor's remarks as "Silly and wild."

Wednesday August 22nd, back in the coalfields there was, indeed, violence. In South Yorkshire the village of Armthorpe and its pit Markham Main colliery were the scenes of the worst violence. Pickets took a crane from the colliery yard and built a barricade with concrete blocks. The village was sealed off by police who claimed that passing vehicles were being stoned. Three men, none of which resided in Armthorpe, had returned to work at Markham Main the previous day and the police response to the build up of pickets at the colliery on Tuesday was to set an ambush. Police lay in wait in the village and the surrounding woodland in order to trap any pickets fleeing from the colliery, where fifty two transit vanloads of police were deployed. Police rampaged through the village in pursuit of miners and they made twenty two arrests. Many pickets were injured and the chase continued into the woods. Police reinforced by Manchester metropolitan officers overreacted savagely, allegedly denying injured men medical treatment. As the police turned Armthorpe into occupied territory, they invaded some homes, one woman suffered extensive facial injuries when police trapped her head in her own back door. Another young woman, Mrs Margaret Paul, at home with only her baby had her window broken. She was not connected with the strike, but was the wife of a council worker, she witnessed six police officers beating a picket. When she approached the thirty or so officers outside her house she was sworn at, she was unable to positively identify the officer responsible for breaking her window as they were not displaying warrant numbers. The best thing that can be said about the Armthorpe incident is – if your home is attacked by thugs it would be normal to contact the police. When the attackers are the police – who do you contact? Who do you turn to?

One miner reported for work at Silverwood colliery near Rotherham despite having to pass burning barricades. Pickets hurled missiles as three men went in at Kiveton Park colliery near Rotherham. Two men went back at Allerton Bywater colliery near Leeds, the five hundred pickets at the pit were outnumbered by police who included metropolitan officers in their ranks. Seven returned to the Selby complex, North Yorkshire, which includes Gascoigne Wood.

In the Durham coalfield picket lines had mixed success, they succeeded in thwarting an attempted return to work at Easington colliery, however sixteen COSA members braved a six hundred strong picket line.

In South Wales the threatened withdrawal of safety cover stopped one rebel miner reporting for work at Bedwas colliery near Caerphilly.

Thursday August 23rd, a row which had been simmering for over a week in Scotland boiled over into a Scottish Dock Strike. The BSC used a private firm of tugboat men at their port in Hunterston, Ayrshire to berth the Panamanian Bulk Carrier 'Ostia' which was laden with 95,000 tonnes of foreign coal bound for Ravenscraig steelworks. The TGWU registered dockers immediately walked out. A BSC spokesman said the unloading of the 'Ostia' was in line with a local agreement drawn up on May 16th with the TGWU. Jimmy Gilligan the TGWU Scottish Docks officer said that a 1979 national agreement had been infringed and pointed out "This is not a political strike. We are looking after members of the TGWU not the NUM."

Friday August 24th, Britain lurched into its second national dock strike in just over a month when a TGWU conference called the stoppage by an overwhelming majority. The Transport Secretary Nicholas Ridley said "It is a political strike engineered to support the crumbling miners' dispute."

Week 25 - "Industrial Crisis"

The NCB were claiming more working miners than ever before, one hundred and seventy one had now reported for work in Scotland they said. Safety cover was withdrawn at Frances colliery, Dysart when four men returned to the pit.

The Kent NUM President Malcolm Pitt lost his appeal against conviction for obstructing a police officer at Ramsgate harbour. Pitt was find £100 with £40 costs, following the verdict the Kent leader said, "It confirms our view that the courts are politically biased against the NUM in this dispute."

There were further reports from the NCB that the prolonged stoppage was causing irreparable damage to many pits. The main supplier of coal to Ravenscraig steelworks, Polkemmet colliery in Whitburn, West Lothian was found to be flooded by 13,000,000 gallons of water and the NCB announced closure. The pit had flooded as a result of safety cover having been withdrawn in protest at six strike breakers. It was also announced that a face had been lost at each of two North Derbyshire pits Shirebrook and Markham.

Tuesday August 28th, trouble flared at Easington colliery in the Durham area when police escorted a miner - Paul Wilkinson through pickets. Pickets twice charged police lines and there were eighteen arrests.

Wednesday August 29th, there were another five arrests outside Easington. Six miners turned up for work at Bold colliery near St Helens in Lancashire and police made over twenty arrests.

Thursday August 30th, at 11.30 pm ten vehicles full of miners forced their way through the security post at Port Talbot steelworks and drove to the docks discharge jetty and climbed onto the three cranes. One hundred and three men held the cranes and others stood by ready to react if the one hundred and fifty officers from the South Wales Police and the British Transport Police tried to approach the cranes. Eric Davies of the NUM said the operation was to show solidarity with the dockers and to try to "Bring steelworkers back into the fold."

Meanwhile, there were thirty nine arrests at Newport, Gwent, following an occupation of the town's transporter- bridge. Seizing control of the gondola pickets drove on with a mini bus stocked with enough supplies to last a fortnight. The men took over the bridge with the intention of stopping shipping to Llanwern steelworks via the river Usk. Missiles were dropped on police attempting to retake the bridge, however, reinforcements arrived and Chief Superintendent Fred Wyer using his loudspeaker ordered the men to give up. The occupation ended and the miners surrendered to the police.

The TUC General Council met and agreed to give the NUM support for the blocking of all movement of coal, coke and oil. A meeting between the TUC and NUM leaders was called to establish a united front to put before congress. Difficulties obviously existed between the various unions which had become entangled in the dispute and the NUM had kept the TUC at arms length throughout. In return for support the TUC expected involvement with future developments.

The dock strike continued despite divisions and amid confusion, Immingham, the Humberside port which had been the catalyst of the first strike, this time surprisingly worked on. TGWU docks secretary John Connolly said, "The response to the strike call has not necessarily been the one we have been looking for, but there has been a high degree of positive response and that will be built on over the next few days." The strike appeared to have thrown up its own 'Silver Birch' in the form of Medlock Bibby a Tilbury docker. Bibby led campaigns, firstly for a ballot, then for a return to work. By the end of the week Felixstowe, Sunderland, Portsmouth, South Shields, Harlepool, and Goole as well as Immingham had decided not to strike. Tilbury men had stayed home despite considerable controversy over the outcome of their ballot, there had been confusion caused by a complex motion from shop stewards and claims that dockers did not know which way they were voting. Moss Evans said that he was ready to meet the BSC and the port employers to resolve the dispute.

Margaret Thatcher cancelled her scheduled visit to the Far East because of the industrial situation. For the opposition Deputy Leader Roy Hattersley said, "At last Mrs Thatcher has recognized the gravity of the present industrial crisis. Let us hope that her decision to cancel the trip to the Far East signals a change of heart and that she will now begin to act like a Prime Minister trying to bring the parties together in the coal and dock dispute." Labour's Employment spokesman John Smith said, "I welcome the fact that Mrs Thatcher has recognized there is an industrial crisis in this country. But there would be little point staying at home if she is not going to do anything about it. So far we have had no move for peace whatever from any member of the Government from the Prime Minister downwards, it is high time the Government intervened to get negotiations going."

Week 26 - Brighton - Trades Union Congress

Monday September 3rd, the mass lobby of the Trades Union Congress at Brighton passed without the predicted incident.

A rally at the Level was addressed by Dave Nellist MP and then the six thousand miners and their supporters marched to the conference centre led by twenty one Cortonwood miners who had spent fourteen days marching to Brighton from South Yorkshire. A rally outside the conference centre was chaired by Ken Cameron leader of the Fire Brigades Union and was addressed by Dennis Skinner MP, Moss Evans (TGWU,) Jimmy Airlie (AUEW,) Bill Keys (SOGAT82) and Mrs Betty Heathfield. The demonstration was good humoured and was described by Mr Roger Birch, Chief Constable of Sussex as "Well ordered and peaceful."

Inside the conference hall Arthur Scargill was given a standing ovation after an impassioned speech calling for full support from Congress and announcing the intended resumption of talks with the NCB. Scargill told delegates that they had a simple choice between supporting the miners or of an "Act of betrayal which would stain the movement forever." The NUM President spoke of the hardships being endured by miners and their families, he said "For the first time since 1926 we have had to establish soup kitchens in every mining village in Britain in order to sustain our people. Our people are starving. They are suffering because they are prepared to fight for their very lives and for generations to come."

Referring to picket line violence Scargill said "We have had violence. Is it not an act of violence to threaten to destroy the job of a man and his son and daughter? That is an act of violence to be condemned. It was an act of violence to say to a colliery like Polmaise or Cortonwood one week that it had five or twenty years life, to transfer men there and then within a week to announce its closure. There have been comments about the conduct of miners attending Congress – I hope those people will have the decency to apologise to those miners."

Speaker after speaker were quick to support the NUMs motion, but Eric Hammond (EEPTU) and John Lyons (Engineers and Management Association of Power Workers) were given a hostile reception by delegates when they refused support and were critical of the conduct of the dispute. TUC General Secretary Len Murray urged the electricians, the power engineers and the blast furnace men to discuss their problems with the NUM, "The NUM has come to the General Council for assistance and we cannot repudiate their request we cannot just stand aside." He asked Congress to support the TUC-NUM joint statement, it was carried overwhelmingly. The statement issued by Congress read as follows :-

1. Support for the NUM's objectives of saving pits, jobs and the mining communities.

2. A concerted campaign to raise money to alleviate hardships in the coal fields and to maintain the union financially.

3. To make the dispute more effective by A) not moving coal or coke, or oil substituted for coal or coke, across NUM official picket lines. B) Not using oil which is substituted for coal.

The NUM acknowledge that the practical implementation of these points will need detailed discussions with the General Council and agreement with unions who would be directly concerned.

The General Council, call for a fresh commitment of all to an expanding coal industry. The General Council call on the NCB to resume negotiations immediately with the NUM to resolve this damaging and costly dispute in line with the Plan for Coal.

Tuesday September 4th, Neil Kinnock addressed Congress he attacked the violence on the miners' picket lines as "The only bone of an excuse" that the government could "gnaw on." He said "It has enabled them to evade their central responsibility for promoting the settlement of the dispute. Kinnock who always seemed to be on a hiding to nothing in these situations went on to give a detailed argument for the miners' case and he received a two minute standing ovation.

On the day that the Leader of the Opposition addressed the TUC, Kent saw conflict as the back-to-work move organised to coincide with Congress spread for the first time into the previously solid coalfield. Twenty four miners reported for work at Tilmanstone colliery. Police outnumbered the two hundred pickets by two to one and they made twenty arrests. Five men reported for work at the nearby Betteshanger colliery. Safety cover was withdrawn at both pits and NACODS members refused to cross the picket lines. The latest round of peace talks were, not for the first time, convened amid total confusion, apparently when Mr Robert Maxwell the millionaire proprietor of the Daily Mirror and former Labour MP had entered the stage as mediator and helped to broker the peace initiative. Mr Ned Smith NCB Industrial Relations telephoned Peter Heathfield and cancelled the talks. This was followed by claim and counterclaim and accusations of lying from both sides. Arthur Scargill told a press conference he was "absolutely disgusted" and went on to allege that Margaret Thatcher must have had a hand in the board's decision. The NUM President also accused Ian MacGregor of lying on television – he had confirmed that the talks were on during an interview with the BBC's 'Newsnight' programme. The NCB's public image was dented by the row and they were not long in offering new talks to commence on Sunday September 9th, Ned Smith offered talks in a letter to Peter Heathfield, with a more open agenda answering a pre-condition imposed by Arthur Scargill.

Thursday September 6th, Kellingley colliery in Yorkshire was the scene of violence when three thousand pickets gathered in an attempt to prevent two working miners from going in. Local NUM officials blamed the police for provoking trouble. Police used truncheons and pickets hurled missiles at the police ranks which numbered two thousand, five hundred. Nine police and four pickets were hurt in the clash and there were four arrests. An Independent Television News van was overturned, vandalised and set on fire. This act was condemned by Kellingley's NUM Secretary David Millar who said that frustration with the news coverage would be better directed against the editors and not the film crews.

Trouble flared elsewhere in the coalfields with another three arrests outside Tilmanstone colliery near Eythorne in Kent. There were nine arrests outside Whitwell colliery, North Derbyshire and six outside Shirebrook colliery in the same coalfield. Eight pickets were arrested when three thousand descended on Kiveton Park colliery in South Yorkshire where smoke bombs and missiles were thrown at police.

Saturday September 8th, Arthur Scargill speaking to a two thousand strong rally at Dinnington, South Yorkshire called on steelworkers and power workers not to cross NUM picket lines, he was accompanied on the platform by Tony Benn MP.

Picketing had been stepped up in the Dock Strike, but strikers failed in their attempt to bring out the key container port of Felixstowe. John Connolly said in Brighton that the strike would go on despite "The problem with many of our members." Nationally seven thousand, seven hundred and eighty dockers were reported to be on strike with six thousand two hundred and sixty still working.

Week 27 - End Of The Second Dock Strike - Imminent

The week was dominated by the talks which had been arranged for Sunday September 9th. They began in a hotel at Edinburgh and lasted through varying degrees of optimism until their breakdown in London on Friday September 14th.

As always the talks were accompanied by their share of complications and drama. There was concern that the talks would quickly collapse, but they in fact took the occasional upturn and at times it looked as if progress was being made. The Edinburgh talks were adjourned with both sides pleading media harassment and so they were re-convened firstly in Yorkshire and then in London. The talks failed when the NUM rejected a third draft of Clause 3c which read "It is agreed that since the advent of the Plan for Coal, there have been colliery closures which do not fall within the definitions of exhaustion or safety, and in accordance with the principles of the plan it is acknowledged that the procedure will continue to apply. In the event of a colliery where a report of an examination by the respective NCB and NUM qualified mining engineers establishes there are no further reserves which can be developed to provide the board in line with their responsibilities, with a basis for continuing operations, there will be agreement between the board and the union that such a colliery be deemed exhausted."

"In line with their responsibilities" was considered to be unacceptable because it left room for pit closures on economic grounds. When the talks ended Messrs Scargill, McGahey and Heathfield left for Congress House where talks which were to last five hours ensued with TUC leaders, namely, Norman Willis the new General Secretary who had taken over from Len Murray who had retired the previous week, David Basnett (GMBTU) and Ray Buckton (ASLEF.) Following the meeting Norman Willis said the TUC was "extremely concerned" and were available "To assist in achieving a return to negotiations and a settlement."

Speaking in divided Nottinghamshire territory to the Bassetlaw Conservative Association the Home Secretary Leon Brittan praised the police for their handling of the dispute and he told the meeting that severe penalties could be handed out for serious offences. He said "Jackboot methods have no place in this country and that neither the government nor the public will allow freedom under the law to be crushed." Joe Ashton the Labour MP for Bassetlaw denounced the Home Secretary's remarks by saying "Leon Brittan has carefully chosen his time and place to cause maximum ill will between the two sides just as Ian MacGregor chose Cortonwood to trigger off this strike. This is the best diversionary tactic the Tories have had to keep attention away from the sinking pound and other problems. They are terrified it might end." The Opposition Home Affairs Spokesman Gerald Kaufmann said on BBC radio "It was not trade unionists wearing jackboots, but people carrying out the orders of a right wing government." Mr Kaufmann added that Brittan's speech had been an attempt to put pressure on the courts.

Wednesday September 12th, a special delegate conference of the pit deputies' union NACODS held in Doncaster decided to call a national ballot with a strike recommendation because of a NCB directive, that NACODS members would not be paid unless they showed a willingness to cross NUM picket lines even if they have to be transported by police.

The South Wales police claimed they had found a petrol bomb after an eight hundred strong picket line at British Benzol coking works at Bedwas, the NUM disclaimed responsibility.

The Chairman of the Police Federation, Mr Leslie Curtis hit out at picket line violence when he addressed the federation at Llandudno, North Wales. He said, "It is even worse than the inner city riots of 1981 because they were not planned or masterminded, and the police were able to restore order and normality quickly."

Ian MacGregor issued an ultimatum to the NUM "The union has to put an end to organised violence. It has to happen before there can be any more negotiations."

As the week ended a settlement in the dock strike looked imminent. The steel unions and dockers in a meeting with opposition transport spokesman, John Prescott and Motherwell Labour MP, Dr Jeremy Bray reached agreement on coal quotas for Ravenscraig steelworks. The agreement still needed the approval of BSC management.

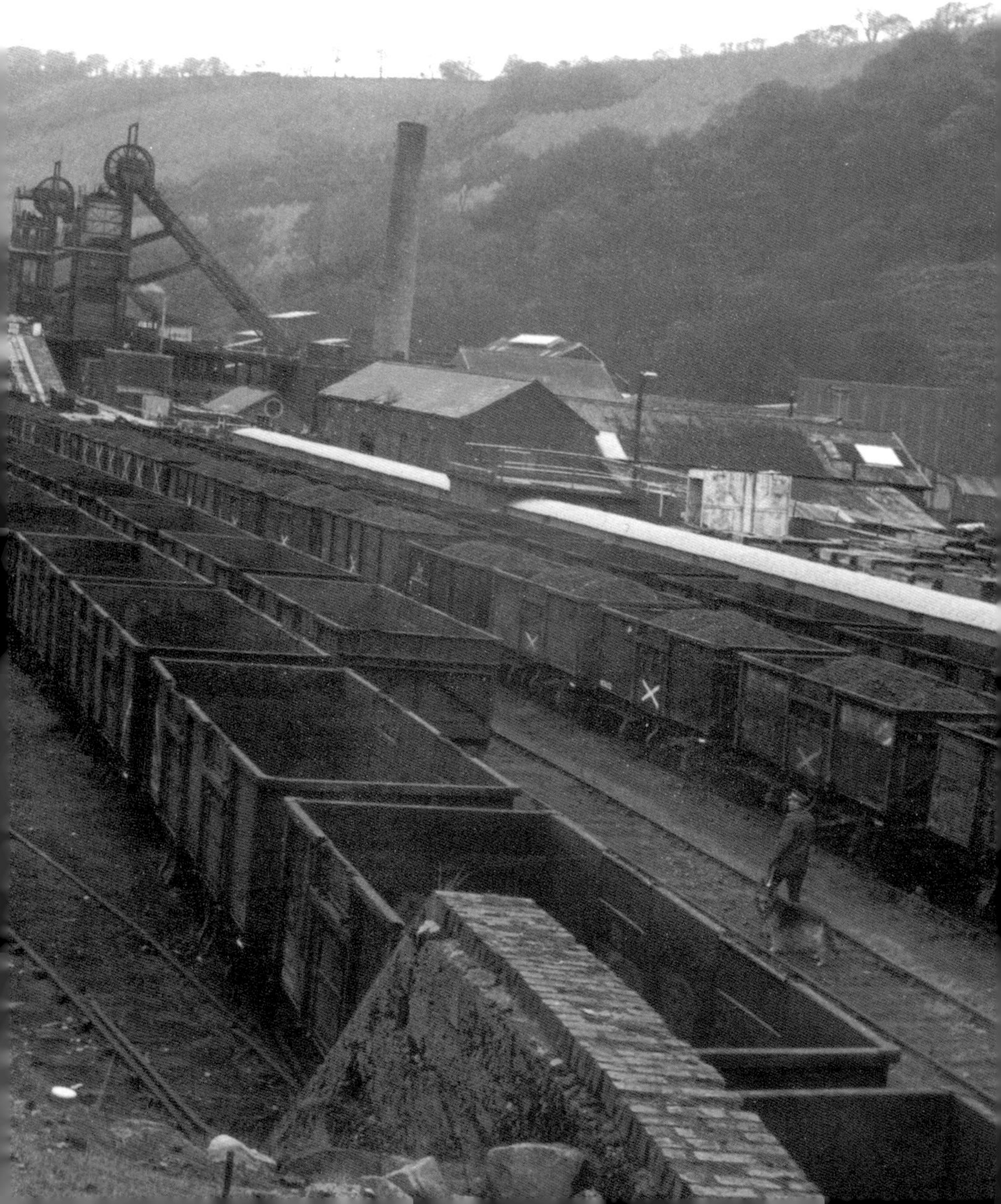

Week 28 - Divine Intervention

Tuesday September 18th, the dock strike ended and ports returned to normal when an agreement for coal quotas for Ravenscraig was agreed, however, the TGWU had to compromise on its original plan for 18,800 tonnes a week by agreeing to increase this to 20,000 tonnes after four weeks and to 22,500 tonnes after eight weeks. Arthur Scargill was not happy with the dockers' deal "We do not expect anyone to make deals which will result in people crossing our picket lines," he said when arriving at a meeting with the transport unions in London.

There were renewed attacks from the Government against the NUM. On BBC radio Margaret Thatcher said, "If the strike goes on for a year or even longer than a year uneconomic pits will have to be closed. All governments have done it in the past and it will have to be done again." Norman Tebbitt speaking to American Bankers at the Chase Manhattan Bank, New York said, "I hope that those who have been wrong about industrial Britain have taken note of the fact that the second attempt to organise a dock strike in support of the Scargill wing of the NUM was defeated by the dockers themselves. Some of the dock workers contented themselves with continuing at work. Some spiced that approach by shouting down the leaders of the union as they went into work. Some voted to work, but were intimidated into staying sullenly at home. Only a tiny minority were enthusiastic supporters of striking on behalf of the Scargillite wing of the NUM." Tuesday September 18th, eight men were escorted by police into work at Kiveton Park colliery South Yorkshire. Six men were arrested as mounted police forced back a crowd estimated as being three thousand, five hundred strong. There had been six arrests earlier at the home of one of the scabs after about two hundred pickets had gathered to protest against his strike breaking.

Thursday September 20th, North Derbyshire NUM conceded in the High Court that it would not discipline three working miners who were awarded injunctions to that effect. The Durham Mechanics section of the NUM expelled three members for crossing the picket line at Wearmouth colliery, Sunderland. The Mechanics' Secretary Billy Etherington said, "We do not really want members who are not prepared to accede to democratic decisions. These three men will have to purge their conscience before they will have any chance of becoming NUM members again."

Friday September 21st, there were violent clashes at Maltby colliery South Yorkshire, five pickets were arrested and two were injured, three policemen were also hurt. A mass picket estimated at six thousand had gathered in an attempt to prevent seven construction workers employed by a contractor going in to

1984 - The Great Coal Strike — Divine Intervention

carry out development work at the pit. The week ended with the new Bishop of Durham telling the congregation at his enthronement ceremony in the city's Cathedral, that the miners must not be defeated. The Right Reverend Professor David Jenkins whose appointment as Bishop had provoked controversy in The Church of England because of his views on the Resurrection and The Virgin Birth, stepped into fresh controversy when he said, "The withdrawal of an imported, elderly American to leave a reconciling opportunity for some local products is neither dishonourable nor improper." The Bishop went on to call for compromise from Mr Scargill to compliment his suggested withdrawal of Mr MacGregor in order to settle the dispute. As the Bishop stepped into a political storm he raised an issue which was to run and run.

MINERS ORGANISE FOR VICTORY

PUBLIC MEETING

SPEAKERS – **EMLYN WILLIAMS, DES DUTFIELD, RON DAVIES** MP **DAFYDD ELLIS THOMAS** MP

7.30 PM. FRI. SEP. 21 ST.
CAERFFILI WORKMEN'S HALL

RHYMNEY VALLEY MINERS SUPPORT GROUP

FREE TRANSPORT TO THE MEETING IS AVAILABLE FOR ALL STRIKING MINERS. BUSES WILL RUN

FROM RHYMNEY (Community Centre) at 6.30pm., via Pontlottyn, Bargoed, etc.
        GELLIGAER (Church) at 6.45pm., via Penybryn, Cefn Hengoed, etc.
        SENGHENYDD (Square) at 6.50pm., via Abertridwr, Penyrheol, Trecenydd.
        GRAIG-Y-RHACCA (Comm. Centre) at 6.50pm., via Trethomas and Bedwas.

AND BACK, AT THE END OF THE MEETING, (At approximately 10.00pm).

Week 29 - Flashpoint - Maltby

The intervention of the Bishop of Durham caused a major political row, bringing attacks from Conservatives, but drew support from other leading figures in the Church and perhaps more predictably from Arthur Scargill. The Energy Secretary Peter Walker led the attack by saying "I was surprised to hear that in a Christian's view there was something wrong with being either elderly or American. I hope before he preaches his next sermon on this topic he takes the trouble to study the facts instead of pronouncing on fiction." The Chairman of the Conservative Party John Selwyn Gummer MP, himself a lay member of the Church of England General Synod questioned the Bishop's partiality.

Harvey Proctor the right-wing Conservative MP for Billericay said "Working and intimidated miners are no less Christian because they march against Scargill and Durham's banner." Nicholas Fairbairn MP (Conservative-Perth and Kinross) was even more forthright, he said "If he wishes to worship earthly gods like Arthur Scargill, let him forsake the post to which he has just been wrongly appointed," then quoting Henry II he asked "Who will rid me of this turbulent priest?"

The Archbishop of Canterbury, Dr Robert Runcie defended Bishop Jenkins. He said it was "A robust statement about reconciliation which all would agree is central to the Gospel message." Support also came from other Anglican Bishops including the Bishops of Wakefield, Winchester, Gloucester and Sheffield. The Roman Catholic Archbishop of Liverpool Monsignor Derek Worlock reinforced Bishop Jenkins' criticisms, speaking in the Isle of Man, he said "Do not write off the current miners' dispute as the mere intransigence of two strong willed men. It is but a symptom of the post-industrial age. What is to happen to whole communities when the industry about which their lives have been bound up and upon which their livelihood has depended is judged to be no longer profitable, practical or even the best way of doing things? That is why this matter concerns us all, why the whole nation needs to take a very clear look about it as we move towards the eleventh hour of the industrial era."

Commenting on the Bishop of Durham's sermon Arthur Scargill said "I believe that in saying the miners must not be defeated he is echoing the sentiments and thoughts of many thousands of British people."

Peter Walker even went to the trouble of writing to Bishop Jenkins asking him to examine the facts. The more the government tried to stifle the issue the longer it was guaranteed to run.

Monday September 24th, Maltby colliery, South Yorkshire – three and a half hours of clashes between an estimated four thousand pickets and the police saw

Kevin Barron the Labour MP for Rother Valley among the four demonstrators who were injured. Mr Barron who later made a complaint against the police to the Chief Constable Mr Peter Wright said he had been attacked without provocation by police wearing boiler suits without warrant numbers. The MP received arm injuries which required hospital treatment and necessitated him wearing a sling after he had been hit during a baton charge. Barron said "There was no attempt to arrest me or anybody else. They were just lacing into people." A journalist received head injuries, fourteen policemen were injured and there were ten arrests.

In South Wales, miners were accused by Mr Viv Brook the Assistant Chief Constable of South Wales Police of dropping missiles from motorway bridges along the M4 on to the convoys travelling between Port Talbot and Llanwern. The Area NUM denied that any of its members were involved.

Tuesday September 25th, at Yorkshire Main colliery near Doncaster some five hundred pickets were confronted by an equal number of police and there were three arrests.

The High Court deferred a ruling on forcing the NUM to hold a national ballot, when the union, represented in court for the first time in a case brought by working miners, said it was prepared to undergo a full trial. The case was brought by working miners from Manton colliery, (geographically in Nottinghamshire, but administratively in Yorkshire) Messrs Bob Taylor and Ken Foulstone. At the end of the four day hearing the coal strike was declared to be illegal. This led to a statement from Arthur Scargill on TV, when on Channel 4 news he said the strike was official and it remained official.

Amid peace initiatives from the Labour Party and the TUC, the Labour Party National Executive threw its weight behind the miners. It was decided that Tony Benn would present a statement to the party conference in Blackpool endorsing the union's fight for jobs and mining communities, but would avoid a reference to either the national ballot or picket line violence. Neil Kinnock had met Arthur Scargill earlier in the week at the Leader of the Opposition's room in the House of Commons, Stan Orme, Mick McGahey and Peter Heathfield, were also present.

Friday September 28th, the result of the NACODS ballot was announced with 82.5% in favour of taking strike action.

Week 30 - Blackpool - Labour Party Conference

Blackpool moved to the centre of the stage as venue of the Labour Party conference. Monday October 1st, the Labour Party Conference gave the miners overwhelming support Stan Orme who had worked so hard behind the scenes to promote peace initiatives throughout the dispute, tried to keep a possible settlement alive in what was at times an acrimonious debate. Orme told conference that he had put forward a suggestion intended to settle the issue of what constitutes an uneconomic pit, but while it had been acceptable to the NUM it had been acceptable to neither the NCB nor the Government. "This is due to the government who do not want a solution to the dispute" he said.

Eric Hammond (EEPTU,) who had been the villain of the peace at the TUC in Brighton, was shouted down by delegates and Party Chairman Eric Heffer MP for Liverpool-Walton had to intervene to restore order. Hammond opposed a motion which had been moved by Arthur Scargill. The electricians' leader was booed and hissed at when he said that it was "Shameful that there was no demand for violence and hooliganism on the picket line to be stopped."

Arthur Scargill, on the other hand, received a hero's welcome. During his speech Scargill said "There are no uneconomic pits. There are only pits which have been deliberately starved of investment. It is obvious to anybody looking at this industry." He said that if there was a surplus of coal "We can begin to practise compassion and give it to the old age pensioners." The NUM President received a two minute standing ovation.

Tony Benn called the dispute "A Titanic Struggle," when winding up the debate on behalf of Labour's National Executive, only a handful of delegates voted against the NUM's call for support.

Later in the day as Arthur Scargill was listening to the debate on the re-selection of MPs he was served with a writ. The writ ordered him to appear before Mr Justice Nicholls and it asked for his committal to Pentonville Prison or the sequestration of the union's funds. Mick McGahey and Peter Heathfield were also served with writs outside the conference hall. Delegates were informed only when chairman, Eric Heffer interrupted the proceedings to make an announcement, he said it was an "absolute scandal" that unauthorised persons should be able to gain access to the conference hall.

Tuesday October 2nd, Neil Kinnock's keynote speech to conference was well received earning him a standing ovation and restoring his authority as party leader. His authority had been badly dented on the previous day in the debate on the re-selection of Labour MPs. Kinnock dealt in depth with the miner's strike and he called on the NUM to stay within the law. "We cannot sharpen legality as our main weapon for the future and then scorn legality because it doesn't suit us at the present time." He criticised the introduction of "National Policing" and he called the coal strike "The product of Thatcherism, the combination of ignorance and arrogance of pride and prejudice, that now rules and overrules this country," he continued "Families and communities in the coalfields know that pit closures would trap them and entomb them in unemployment and deprivation for all of the foreseeable future. They know that under Thatcherism no alternatives exist and none are coming. That is why the resistance has been so determined. People who don't comprehend it should understand that these communities are like someone fighting for air to breathe."

Mr Justice Nicholls ruled in the High Court that Arthur Scargill's televised remarks about the legality of the strike were in contempt of court. Scargill was not represented in court and the proceedings were adjourned for six days, to, in the words of the judge "Give the NUM and its President time to reflect further on their position and to consider the desirability of their being represented at the adjourned hearing." The two working Yorkshire miners Taylor and Foulstone were joined in court by 'Silver Birch' Chris Butcher. Earlier in the week Foulstone and Taylor had been escorted by police through the picket line into Manton colliery when there were twenty three arrests.

Scargill's reaction to the High Court ruling was typically defiant when he told a conference fringe meeting organised by Labour Briefing that he was prepared to go to gaol. A second writ was subsequently served on the NUM President relating to comments he had made in the Times.

As the Labour Party met in Blackpool, the Chairman of the Police Federation, Leslie Curtis told a meeting of the Federation in Hull that the police maybe unable to work with the future Labour Government, in his speech he said, "I hope that away from the emotion of Blackpool and the Party militants, the Labour leadership will realise that the decisions taken last Monday have undermined police confidence in the intentions of a future Labour Government." He went on to say that the police service had always been able to offer both Labour and Conservative Home Secretaries the same loyal service, "Now for the first time in police history that system which has been a major factor in ensuring the political neutrality of the police service is under threat." During the dispute much has been made of certain union leaders posing a threat to democracy, now we had the Chairman of the Police Federation making an unequivocal threat. The Bishop of Durham, Professor David Jenkins replied to Peter Walker's letter by saying that if the strike continued the miners, the Government and the country would be defeated.

In South Yorkshire there was further confrontation at both Kiveton Park and

Rossington collieries. The week ended with NACODS meeting the NCB with the NUM at ACAS. NACODS negotiating with an 82.5% strike mandate had proposed a peace formula for the miners' strike with an independent 3rd party to arbitrate on pit closures.

Week 31 - Brighton - Conservative Party Conference

Friday October 12th, the events of the week in the dispute were overshadowed by the tragically 'unreal' circumstances immediately preceding the finale of the Conservative Party Conference at Brighton.

Five leading Conservatives lost their lives in an explosion caused by an IRA bomb at the Grand Hotel Brighton. Sir Anthony Berry the MP for Enfield Southgate was one of those killed. Mr John Wakeman the Government Chief Whip and Mr Norman Tebbitt were amongst the injured. The bomb outrage had been an attempt to assassinate the Prime Minister and her whole Cabinet.

The miners' strike had of course received an airing at the conference. But even before the conference began Norman Tebbitt and Peter Heathfield had crossed swords over the proposed peace initiative. Following exploratory talks between Messrs Heathfield and Scargill with ACAS, Peter Heathfield commenting on the, "constructive and helpful meeting" said, "I think that from the form of words being knocked about over the weekend there is a possibility of ending the dispute, providing there is willingness on the part of Margaret Thatcher to allow Ian MacGregor to end the dispute." Tebbitt interpreted this to mean that the NUM were prepared to move ground on pit closures. Heathfield later retorted, "There's been no change at all in the NUM's position, to suggest after thirty weeks that we would suddenly accept something that caused the strike is preposterous."

At the conference the dispute featured prominently in the Law and Order debate. Opening the debate Mr William Coates (Meriden) said, "Two of the five key principles of our manifesto were to protect and strengthen law and order. I believe that we have failed to honour these commitments. We have let the moderate miners down and we have let the police down."

"On the cost of the strike we must be mad to allow the tax and rate payer to carry this burden - I believe that social security payments to strikers' families should be abolished, and unions should pay the costs of policing their own picket lines."

Turning to the policing of the strike Mr Eldon Griffiths Parliamentary advisor to the Police Federation attacked anti-police views which had been expressed by some delegates at the Labour Party Conference. "There is no such thing as a Conservative Policeman any more than there are "Tory Judges" he said, and then followed this extraordinary claim by saying "The miner's strike has stoked up Labour's malevolence against the Police to unprecedented levels of vituperation and for the first time overt violence and illegality. But this is only the tip of the iceberg. The hard left has been running its anti-police campaign for most of the past fifteen years."

Winding up the debate the Home Secretary Mr Leon Brittan said, "The police have received the Government's total support. They will continue to do so."

The Church of England's Chairman of the General Synod's Board for Social Responsibility, The Bishop of Birmingham, Dr. Hugh Montefiore joined the chorus of Church leaders when he called for, "A new creative start" to peace talks in a bid to end the dispute.

On Wednesday October 10th, instead of attending the High Court to answer the charge of contempt, Arthur Scargill reported for duty at the union's HQ in Sheffield. In his absence the union was fined £200,000 with fourteen days to pay and the President was personally fined £1000 and he was given twenty eight days to pay. In fining the NUM and its President, Mr Justice Nicholls said, "A great and powerful trade union with a large membership has decided to regard itself as above the law." Defiantly Arthur Scargill read a prepared statement to waiting journalists from the steps of the NUM offices. "The NUM national coordinating committee which acts on a day to day basis on behalf of The National Executive, reaffirms the decision taken by the National Executive last Monday as the official policy of the union. This means that the strike action in the British coalfield is official in accordance with Nation Rule 41. The union will continue to do all in its power to win maximum support for the strike and reaffirms that there should be no crossing of official picket lines of the union."

Later in the week the High Court upheld bail conditions imposed by Nottinghamshire magistrates on nine Yorkshire miners. The Lord Chief Justice Lord Lane passing judgement said, "By the time these defendants appeared in court it must have been clear to everyone and to the magistrates in particular, that any suggestion of peaceful picketing was a colourful pretence and that it was a question of picketing by intimidation and threat." The bail conditions which had been challenged restricted the nine men from picketing anywhere other than their own place of work.

As blows rained down on the NUM from all directions, NUM National Executive member Roy Ottey, General Secretary of the union's power group and a leading moderate resigned a month before his 60th birthday. Ottey, a magistrate, took his decision because of his unwillingness to break the law.

Week 32 - Flashpoint - Grimethorpe

Monday October 15th, and talks at ACAS between the NCB and NUM/NACODS broke down amid bitter words. Arthur Scargill said Ian MacGregor had wanted to violate the Plan for Coal. NACOD's General Secretary Peter McNestry said, "We've gone as far as we can with the NCB." Both unions decided to consult the respective National Executives.

Tuesday October 16th, the NACODS Executive gave notice of strike action to commence on October 25th. Then hypocrisy of hypocrisies, Peter Walker called on NACODS to ballot again. It would seem that the secret ballot is the jewel of democracy as long as the result goes the Government's way. In any case the NACOD'S decision led to a flurry of activity by the board to find a solution to the deputies' grievance in order to leave the NUM, once again, in isolation.

Embattled South Yorkshire was prominent again, when an attack was made on the village police station at Grimethorpe. Insensitive policing had resulted in twenty two people being arrested for picking coal from the local colliery tip. The picking of coal from NCB property is of course of dubious legality but has long been regarded as a tradition right of striking miners. Local reaction to the arrests culminated in the attack. During the attack two police officers took flight, as youths, some apparently wearing balaclavas, threw stones breaking every window in the police station. The mob pursued two fleeing officers, one of them a police woman, both required hospital treatment after being beaten. A meeting was later held in the local Welfare Hall attended by residents, community leaders and senior police officers in an attempt to defuse the situation.

The week also saw violence at Rossington colliery near Doncaster and at Wooley colliery near Barnsley (the pit where the young Arthur Scargill had began his mining career.) At Tow Law, County Durham, twelve policemen were slightly injured as about seven hundred pickets tried to prevent the movement of coal from an open cast site.

An anonymous donor paid the outstanding £1000 fine imposed for contempt on Arthur Scargill. "It has been done without my authority or permission," said the NUM President who had made it clear that he had no intention of ever paying it.

> *Yes, as through this world I've wandered I've seen lots of funny men*
> *Some will rob you with a six gun and some with a fountain pen.*
> (Pretty Boy Floyd) Woody Guthrie 1912-1967.

Week 33 - Sequestration

Michael Eaton the NCB'S North Yorkshire Director who had recently been appointed as the board's chief spokesman on the dispute repeated Peter Walker's call for NACODS to ballot again. The call from Eaton supposedly regarded has having a good working relationship with the unions, brought a terse rebuff from NACODS' Peter McNestry who said that although generally attributed to Ian MacGregor, it was in fact Eaton who was the first area director to stop paying deputies who refused to cross picket lines, it was this decision which at first upset the normally moderate union. On the ballot McNestry said, "Mr Eaton in North Yorkshire decried the NUM for not having a ballot. We had one, democratically conducted, and he is now trying to undermine the fact that we had a ballot."

Wednesday October 24th, on the day before NACODS were due to join the coal dispute, the hedging by the deputies' union stopped when their executive called off the strike. It is believed that the NACODS decision displeased the TUC who preferred a suspension of strike action until the outcome of talks between the NUM and the NCB convened to commence at ACAS the next day. The coal board reached agreement with NACODS in a document which made proposals for a new five year plan reflecting market and production opportunities. The document also contained an agreement to include the five pits which were named for closure on March 6th in the colliery review procedure for consideration, also to reconsider the closure of twenty pits with the loss of 20,000 jobs in consultation with all unions concerned and taking into account the coal output loss resulting from the strike. With no mention of the Plan for Coal and with the reference to market and production opportunities it was difficult to see the NACODS agreement suiting the NUM. The NACODS' settlement was, however, used as the basis of new talks between the NCB and the NUM.

The talks arranged with the assistance of the TUC and ACAS were held under the now customary cloud. As well as the isolation caused by the NACODS' deal earlier in the week while the NACODS/NCB talks were still in progress, Arthur Scargill had called Peter Walker and ACAS chairman Pat Lowry, liars for maintaining only one document was discussed in the previous, unsuccessful round of talks. Scargill made the allegations at Congress House, when he stated that ACAS had produced three documents, two of which were agreeable to the NUM. Lowry discounted the allegations by saying that four documents had been produced, but only one was an ACAS document. Peter Walker said, "That was the one document that the National Coal Board agreed to and the National Union of Mine Workers rejected. The only two documents that Scargill agreed to was the one setting out what ACAS understood to be the NUM's requirements and the one which was headed 'Modifying Suggestions out of discussions with the NUM.'"

Thursday October 25th, the talks made little progress but were adjourned to recommence the next week after both sides were given time by ACAS to prepare further information.

Meanwhile in the High Court the NUM's assets were ordered to be sequestrated because the union had failed to pay its outstanding £200,000 fine. In ordering the sequestration Mr Justice Nicholls said, "I have given the NUM and its officers, clear warning where their wilful disobedience of orders of the court was leading. In my judgement I have given those officers ample opportunity, indeed, more than ample opportunity to put their house in order. But despite that warning and despite that opportunity and despite the serious consequences, still the NUM persist in regarding the law of this country as applicable to others and not to itself. Thus it is to those officers that the members of the NUM should address the question. How can this have happened to our union? What has brought the NUM to the sorry state of having all its properties sequestrated? Is it it's refusal to accept that its members have rights against their union which the law should be ready to protect as the union has rights against its members and others?"

The immediate reaction from the union was for thirty Durham miners to occupy the Sheffield headquarters against any threat from bailiffs acting for the sequestrators – Price Waterhouse, the Birmingham firm of Chartered Accountants who had handled the South Wales Area sequestration. Mrs Anne Scargill and others helped remove files and union documents from the Sheffield office. The day to day financing of the dispute passed to the areas, it is believed that the National Union's assets were in excess of £8,000,000. Anne Scargill had been in the news earlier in the week when on Tuesday October 23rd she and three other women were cleared of charges, by Mansfield Magistrates, relating to alleged offences outside Silverhill colliery Nottinghamshire.

Week 34 - The Libyan Affair

The Sunday Times on October 28th carried the exclusive "Scargill : The Libyan Connection" – the front page story told of the visit by the NUM Chief Executive Roger Windsor the previous week to Tripoli, where he met the Libyan Leader Colonel Gaddafi. The news came as a bombshell and looked as if it would cause irreparable damage to the miners' cause. It would be a difficult task to find a World Leader who could provoke such widespread revulsion, and public support was in danger of being seriously eroded.

The siege in April at the Libyan People's Bureau in London which resulted in the murder of WPC Yvonne Fletcher and the wounding of ten anti-Gaddafi student demonstrators had done little to endear the Libyan Leader to the British people.

The Labour and Trade Union movement was quick to distance itself from the NUM's action and the move was condemned by all political parties. Norman Willis explained that the reason for Roger Windsor's visit was to outline the NUM's case to Trade Unionists in Libya and it transpired that the union had established links with some fifty countries during the dispute. The TUC General Secretary said he had asked for, and been given an assurance by Arthur Scargill that "No financial support has been sought for, received by, or will be accepted by the NUM from the Libyan regime, which he, like myself, regards as an odious tyranny."

"I have expressed to Mr Scargill my condemnation of the meeting with Colonel Gaddafi. This has created the impression that the NUM is prepared to consort with a government which is heavily implicated in terrorist campaigns outside its own borders" said Willis.

Neil Kinnock said "By any measure of political, civil, trade union or human rights, the Gaddafi regime is vile. Any offers from them would be an insult to everything the British trade union movement stands for. If such offers are ever made, then of course they must and will be rejected."

The Liberal Leader David Steel said "The strike is nakedly exposed as political, not industrial."

For the Government Peter Walker said "Now that Mr Scargill has made clear that he is in touch with Libya as well as Russia and Hungary, we must remember the old maxim that you must judge a man by his friends."

The NCB reciprocated with an own goal when Ian MacGregor, coming under widespread criticism for his public handling of the dispute was involved in an internal squabble at Hobart House which culminated in the Director for Information Geoffrey Kirk being given "indefinite leave."

The Libyan affair was demoted in prominence, with the news from New Delhi that the Indian Prime Minister Mrs Indira Ghandi had been assassinated by two members of her Sikh Bodyguard. There were several unsuccessful attempts to resurrect the issue, but the tragic events in India now rightly dominated World news. The Gaddafi affair was gone if not forgotten.

Wednesday October 31st, the coal talks at ACAS broke down and Ian MacGregor said he could see no early resumption of talks.

Thursday November 1st, the NUM executive met at Sheffield for four and a half hours and decided to recall a special delegate conference. It was also agreed to seek further assistance from the TUC and to organise five special rallies and to invite Neil Kinnock and Norman Willis to attend at least one.

A press conference after the meeting, was abruptly terminated by Arthur Scargill when a reporter from Independent Television News, who had earlier interviewed Colonel Gaddafi, tried to press the NUM President on the Libyan affair. Scargill said "You mean you have been talking to people you yourselves have been criticising? You do surprise me." Scargill added, "You will also be aware that the British Government have been importing Libyan oil in order to try to defeat the British miners. We have not received one penny piece from Libya, we have not received food or any other aid from them."

The week also saw renewed legal action, picket line confrontation, and a leaked coal board document. The document from the North East Director to NCB headquarters, outlined plans to close eleven of the area's pits over the next fifteen years. The NCB confirmed its authenticity, but said it was only part of a larger document, and therefore it gave a misleading impression.

Sixteen working miners issued writs seeking that the twenty five individual members of the national executive be made personally liable for the NUM's outstanding £200,000 fine. One of the plaintiffs, working Nottinghamshire miner, Colin Clarke, 'President' of the so-called Working Miners Committee said "The majority of the membership feel that the people who are making these contemptuous remarks should pay the fine. We are not going to be responsible for the bills that these people have incurred."

An electrician returned to work at the Kinsley drift mine near Pontefract, but he rejoined the strike after talking to local union officials. Two policemen were injured during brief scuffles as police dismantled a barricade which the two hundred pickets had erected, two pickets were arrested. Three police officers were also hurt as one miner returned to Wooley colliery.

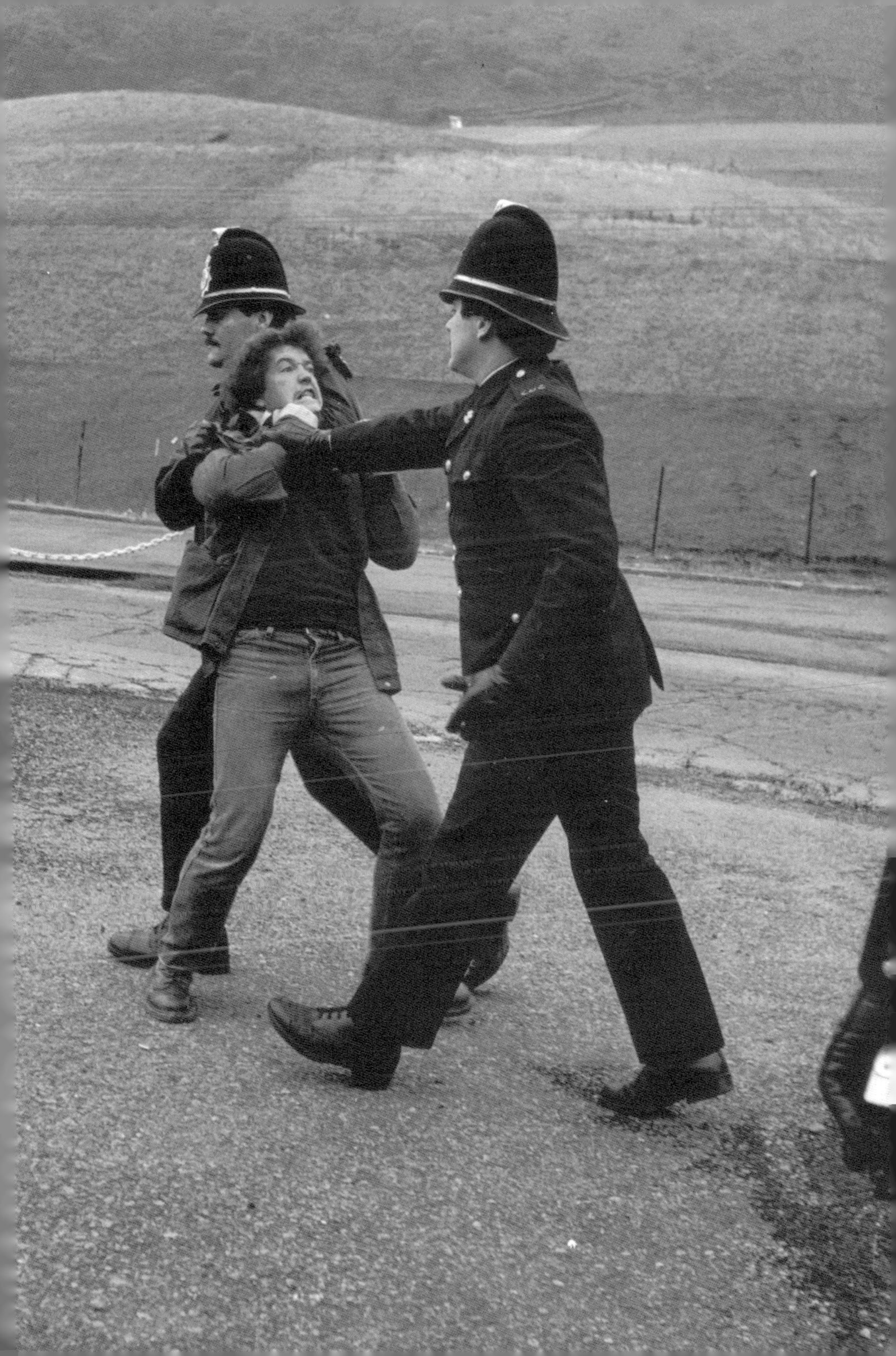

Week 35 - *The Christmas Bonus*

With Christmas just around the corner the NCB played a trump card in an effort to break the strike. An offer of a Christmas pay packet of up to £650 for men returning to work and an individual letter to each of the board's seventeen thousand miners in the Western Area which stated that it had ended all attempts to reach a negotiated settlement to the dispute. The offer which Arthur Scargill called "blackmail" was to cause the first lasting cracks to appear in the solid South Wales coalfield.

The press and media began to give a day by day return to work figure, but the overall figure was the subject of dispute between board and union, and was calculated by disparate means, it would be meaningless to quote. Indisputable was the fact that there was now a considerable drift back to work taking place.

The board had more success in the North East and in North Derbyshire. An estimated seventy men returned to Bersham colliery in North Wales, this prompted a ballot at the pit, by a slender majority the miners voted to continue the strike.

In South Wales local management at Cynheidre colliery near Llanelli had to make alternative arrangement when twenty seven women staged a sit in at the pit-head baths. A total of twenty seven men returned led by a deposed former NUM lodge chairman, Tony Hollman. Paul Watson the husband of a leading back to work campaigner, Mrs Joy Watson, returned to the Phurnacite Smokeless Fuel Plant at Abercwmboi in the Cynon Valley.

In Gwent one COSA member returned to Markham colliery near Blackwood and five men returned at the two Abertillery pits, two at the Abertillery New Mine (Roseheyworth) and three at the neighbouring Six Bells colliery. There were nine arrests for public order offences outside Roseheyworth colliery. One returned at both Cwm colliery, Beddau and at Nant Garw, near Treforrest. At Cwm colliery two policemen were injured as two hundred pickets gathered in an attempt to prevent the return of one Tommy Hughes who had made an abortive attempt in August. Monty Morgan the first miner to attempt to return in South Wales during August left his home near Bridgend, to move to the Tewkesbury area of Gloucestershire. Tensions created by his two attempts to strike break in August were blamed for his need to move house.

The NUM response in South Wales to the trickle back to work was the withdrawal of safety cover.

South Yorkshire again witnessed ugly scenes when five hundred pickets turned out at the catalyst pit Cortonwood colliery, Brampton Brierlow, and clashed with police as a lone miner who was not named was escorted into work.

The NCB back to work drive was likely to create grave social consequences not just during the strike but for years ahead. The picket lines were thinning as the NUM fought a rearguard action, but the police were also being spread in order to cover the newly created situation. Relations between police and public, in the mining communities, were under great strain and were in danger of worsening as they already had in some areas, notably, South Yorkshire. There was speculation that mass picketing was coming to an end, however, Markham colliery in North Derbyshire as well as Whittle colliery, Northumberland and Eppleton colliery, near Sunderland in the Durham area were all scenes of heavy picketing. The unions special delegate conference met in Sheffield and decided there would be no cooperation with the sequestrators.

Week 36 - No Noose Is Good News

Tuesday November 13th, the fourth of the five special rallies went ahead at the Afon Lido, Aberavon, Port Talbot. On this occasion Messrs Scargill, McGahey and Heathfield were joined on the platform by the shadow spokesman for Wales Mr Barrie Jones MP, South Wales President Emlyn Williams, Jim Mortimore The General Secretary of The Labour Party and most significantly Mr Norman Willis.

In contrast to the warm reception given by the rally to the other speakers, Mr Willis was anything but popularly received. What promised to be a well constructed speech was cut short when the General Secretary of the TUC strongly condemned all violence from whatever quarter. Some of the worst violence seen during the dispute had taken place in Yorkshire the previous day at Hickleton colliery near Doncaster where thirty three police and nine pickets were injured and there were forty five arrests. At Dinnington the local police station was evacuated under attack from petrol bombs. Petrol bombs were also used during disturbances in the village of Brampton Brierlow, Cortonwood. Struggling to be heard above the heckling, Mr Willis said, "There have been scenes of unprovoked police aggression, which are utterly alien to the British tradition of policing by consent and it is hypocritical in the extreme for ministers to ignore the evidence of police wrong doing while extracting maximum propaganda value out of their version of the ugly picket line clashes."

A lack of discipline born of frustration at the TUCs' apparent coolness to the strike and their failure to deliver the goods they had packaged at Brighton, led to a noose being dangled in front of Willis. The incident, which undoubtedly had more humour attached to it than the press or media gave credit for, sparked a storm over the next couple of days - Norman Willis was later to accept it philosophically and in a good natured way, saying, "I must say I did not see it as a gesture of support but it wasn't a sinister thing. I did not feel that anyone was about to put it around my neck. I was smiling at the time and so were a lot of people there." Tailor made for television it seems unfortunate that none of the miners' leaders intervened but perhaps Norman Willis would not have wanted it that way.

Later in the week Neil Kinnock said he would arrange to join a picket line and with a change of mind that he would appear on a platform with Arthur Scargill.

The lure of the Christmas bonus saw the drift back to work continue. In South Wales less than 1% of the coalfields miners had returned. In Gwent the two Abertillery pits Six Bells and Roseheyworth, were again strikebound, when the five rebels abandoned their return to work. However, the picket line at another Gwent pit was breached. At times throughout the week the picket line at South Celenyn colliery Newbridge was over five hundred strong and the police used riot gear and on one occasion they made three arrests, nineteen men returned at the pit. Elsewhere in South Wales, one man went back, then later rejoined the strike at Bedwas colliery near Caerphilly. Others returned at Cwm colliery Beddau, and the anthracite pits of Abernant at Pontardawe in the Swansea Valley, Bettws in Ammanford, Cynheidre near Llanelli, Treforgan in the village of Crynant near Neath and Wernos coal preparation plant near Ammanford. In North Wales, more men were reporting for work at Bersham colliery, despite the ballot held the previous week.

Despite solid resistance in South Wales, the NCB were regarding the national return as a success. Predictably the Board decided to extend the final date for returning miners to qualify for the Christmas bonus payment.

At a national Executive meeting in Sheffield Arthur Scargill announced that Stan Orme MP was exploring ways of reopening talks and that the NUM would approach the Church of England to assist in settling the dispute. A joint statement in response to Scargill's call to the churches was issued by the Archbishops of Canterbury and York which read, "Should there be a serious request from the NUM to act in a mediating or reconciling roll we would respond positively in consultation with other Church leaders."

Week 37 - "A Gratuitously Vindictive Act"

A plan being considered by government ministers, to resettle working miners when the strike was over, exposed a communication problem between the NCB and the government. The plan was scrapped as there was a feeling at the coal board that such a scheme would create "Colonies of mining lepers." It is believed that NCB chairman Ian MacGregor had not even been consulted.

In South Wales three miners returned for the first time to another Gwent pit, the Marine colliery, Cwm, near Ebbw Vale, they were taken through the picket line by police who used dogs and riot gear. At one point five men turned up for work, but the figure fell to three by the end of the week. Police investigated an incident when seventy windows were smashed at the colliery premises. There was also an incident which involved police in riot gear, entering a haulier's yard adjoining the colliery site, the haulier's employees were apparently mistaken for pickets.

Three rebels went back to work and then rejoined the strike at Blaenant colliery, Onllwyn West Glamorgan. There was also a first time return at Merthyr Vale colliery near Merthyr Tydfil, which was the scene of violent clashes between pickets and police, four policemen were injured in one incident. Police made four arrests outside the home of a working miner who had returned to Merthyr Vale. There were several other locations which saw arrests and minor incidents, but South Wales remained overwhelmingly solid.

In Yorkshire, police were investigating an attack on a working miner, Mr Michael Fletcher who had returned the previous week to Fryston colliery, Castleford. Mr Fletcher was admitted to hospital in Pontefract suffering from a broken shoulder blade and other injuries. He had been attacked at his Airdale home by men armed with baseball bats.

In the North-East at Easington colliery in the Durham coalfield a return to work was led by the NUM branch Secretary John Cunningham, whose son also named John, remained on strike.

In North Wales the NUM area executive said it could no longer maintain support for the strike following the collapse at Bersham colliery. Ironically Bersham had recently reaffirmed support for the strike by ballot and earlier in the dispute had dissociated itself from the neighbouring Point of Ayr colliery, where one hundred and ten men remained on strike compared with just eighty at Bersham.

Wednesday November 21st, and Parliament witnessed rowdy scenes when Norman Fowler the Social Services Secretary went to the Commons, on the insistence of the opposition, to make a statement on a government decision to change Supplementary Benefits payments to striking miners' families. The decision involved a £1 deduction from benefits. The amount of deemed strike pay was changed from £15 to £16. About thirty Labour backbenchers led by Eric Heffer, disrupted Commons business as Norman Fowler tried to make the statement. During the ensuing commotion one Labour MP Dave Nellist (Coventry South-East) snatched the Minister's statement from the despatch box and tore it up. The demonstration in defiance of the Speaker led to the adjournment of the sitting.

Thursday November 22nd, there were noisy scenes at Prime Minister's Question Time, relating to the incidents of the previous night. Mr Roy Hattersley deputising for Neil Kinnock who was in Moscow, asked Mrs Thatcher to justify the changes in benefit payments. The Prime Minister replied "As for explaining it, the Social Services Secretary tried to and was prevented by the rowdiest scenes this House has ever seen perpetrated by Labour MPs." Labour's Deputy Leader then accused her of a "Gratuitously vindictive act." In response Margaret Thatcher said "The callousness and vindictiveness should be turned on those in the NUM who are prepared to use the money for mob violence rather than for paying for those that are on strike." The Prime Minister went on to explain that the increases arose from the formula contained in the Social Security Act of 1980. Following a noisy debate the Speaker made a statement to the House, he said "For centuries this House has seen the strongest expression of conflicting opinion and policy. And over the centuries this House has jealously guarded its procedure of free debate. I remind the House that if its proceedings are brought to a halt by disorderly conduct, and this does include refusal to hear the opinions of others, then this long tradition is damaged and violated and the authority of Parliament is undermined."

Week 38 - The Price Of Coal

The NUM Christmas appeal received a boost from an unexpected quarter when the multi-millionaire Mr John Paul Getty Jnr Donated £100,000. In defiance of the Attorney General's guidelines on Student Union expenditure, North London Polytechnic Students' Union made a donation of £1,000 to two support groups in County Durham.

Thursday November 29th, on the M4 motorway near Bridgend, police made twenty eight arrests following stone throwing at lorries travelling between Port Talbot and Llanwern.

There were eleven arrests and two policemen injured, as an estimated four hundred pickets tried to stop a taxi taking two miners to work at Merthyr Vale colliery near Merthyr Tydfil.

Friday November 30th, the South Wales coalfield was shocked and saddened with an event which was to cast a cloud over the strike. Mr David Wilkie aged 35, a taxi driver from Treforest, who was an employee of Cardiff firm City Centre Cars, was killed as he drove a working miner, David Williams to Merthyr Vale colliery. Mr Wilkie was killed when a three feet long concrete post and an eighteen inch block of concrete smashed through the taxi windscreen pinning the driver to his seat whilst the car spun out of control careering up a roadside bank. The incident happened on the A465 Heads of the Valleys road at Rhymney Bridge, Rhymney, Mid-Glamorgan. The passenger David Williams escaped unhurt. Mr Wilkie was cut free from the wreckage, but was pronounced dead on arrival at Prince Charles Hospital Merthyr Tydfil. As South Wales Police launched a massive operation, Chief Constable David East said "This is not industrial action, this is not picketing. This is murder." Speaking on behalf of the South Wales NUM, Dr Kim Howells said "I feel a sense of great sorrow and dismay at what has happened. It is a tragedy of the worst kind and we have all been knocked flat. We feel nothing but tragedy and grief for the man's family and a sense of revulsion at what has happened. But I think it was inevitable that some kind of tragedy would occur because of the way in which the coalfield has been wound up in the past few weeks. We have easily been the most disciplined coalfield in Britain, but in the past two weeks we have seen an attempt by the coal board to get people back into the pits, and the communities themselves have been split wide open."

Arthur Scargill appearing on the same platform as Neil Kinnock at Stoke-on-Trent that night dissociated the NUM from the tragic incident when he said "As President of the NUM, it is incumbent on me to make reference to events that took place this morning. I want to make it clear, on behalf of the NUM that we are deeply shocked by the tragedy this morning which resulted in the death of a South Wales taxi driver, Mr Wilkie." The miners' leader condemned acts of violence which occur "away from the picket line." The rally gave the NUM President a standing ovation. Neil Kinnock, however, received a mixed reception and the start of his speech was delayed by five minutes of cheering and jeering, the Labour Party leader said "The violence has got to stop and stop now."

Saturday December 1st, two men – Reginald Dean Hancock aged 21, of Rhymney, a miner employed at Oakdale colliery, Gwent and Russell Shankland aged 20, of Rhymney, a miner employed at Taff Merthyr colliery, Mid-Glamorgan appeared before Merthyr Tydfil Magistrates Court charged with murder. They were remanded in custody.

In a small mining community, a time like this produces strong emotions and the community of Merthyr Vale know only too well the price which can be paid for coal, for it was in the neighbouring hamlet of Aberfan on that terrible day in October 1966, that a generation of school children were killed when one of Merthyr Vale's coal tips slipped, spilling its black slurry on the village school below. At the Aberfan Tribunal, the then NCB chairman Lord Robens took full responsibility for the disaster. Now eighteen years later their cynical policies must share in the responsibility which led to the Rhymney tragedy.

A total of eighteen miners appeared during two separate hearings before Pontefract Magistrates Court on various charges connected to the attack on Michael Fletcher at his home the previous week. Of those charged eleven were remanded in custody and seven were allowed conditional bail.

Arthur Scargill was absent from NUM/TUC talks, trying to find a peace formula. Mick McGahey and Peter Heathfield met TUC leaders at Congress House. A subsequent meeting of the NUM national executive at Sheffield was critical of the lack of information about the TUC talks, on this occasion Arthur Scargill was present, but the two other members of the union's negotiating team were absent on other union business. Mick McGahey at a rally in Scotland and Peter Heathfield at legal proceedings in London, this was the first time any of the union's national officers had appeared personally in the High Court during the strike. In a short statement following the Sheffield meeting Arthur Scargill described the NCB's back-to-work campaign as "abysmal."

Week 39 - The Receiver

Both miners and the police observed two minutes silence on the picket line outside Merthyr Vale colliery as a mark of respect for all those who had died during the coal strike.

Mr Horace Brewer, a Derbyshire solicitor, a former Conservative councillor and a member of the Institute of Directors was appointed by the high court to act as receiver and to run the NUM's affairs. The union's response was to call an emergency delegate conference in London.

Meanwhile, Mr Brewer left Heathrow Airport for Luxembourg where the sequestrators Price-Waterhouse had located £4.63 million which had been frozen and then released by a court in the Grand Duchy. Other union funds located were £2.78 million frozen in a bank in The Republic of Ireland. In Luxembourg, Mr Brewer failed to obtain the funds from Nobis-Finanz Bank and so he returned to Britain later in the week.

The emergency delegate conference lasted for seventy five minutes, and gave Arthur Scargill a mandate to refuse co-operation with both the law and with the receiver. The conference also called on the TUC to organise industrial action to defend the threat to the freedom of trade unions. After the conference, Scargill met with Norman Willis at Congress House in an effort to obtain further financial assistance and an alternative accommodation in the event of the NUM Sheffield headquarters being seized.

Interviewed on Channel 4 television, Arthur Scargill said he believed the action of the High Court was the prelude to smashing the whole trade union movement. "I only hope that trade unions recognise that they now have to stand up and fight." He said. When asked how he intended to run the union without funds, he replied, "Like the Tolpuddle Martyrs, with difficulty but with success. I think we will have some money from our friends in the national and international trade union and labour movement, I don't accept we will be on our own at all. I would have thought that there would probably be more determination on the part of miners already out on strike to stay out on strike and to encourage those not on strike to come out on strike."

Thursday December 6th, the TUC and the NUM met at Congress House, but the TUC informed the miners' representatives that while it would consider any method in which it could assist the NUM it would not entertain any measures likely to lay itself open to charges of contempt of court. Taking legal advice from its own lawyers, the TUC stressed that if it offered the NUM new premises from which to operate, running costs and staff wages it would leave itself wide open to contempt charges. Following the meeting which lasted six hours, Scargill said that the TUC had reiterated its support and would do everything it could to assist the NUM.

Horace Brewer, frustrated in his efforts to obtain the NUM funds, decided to stand down as receiver. In his place the court appointed Mr Michael John Arnold senior insolvency partner in the London based firm of accountants - Arthur Young, McClelland, Moore and Company, he was the choice of the Counsel acting on behalf of the sixteen working miners.

Neil Kinnock was well received when he addressed the NUM's Oakdale colliery Lodge in his Islwyn constituency. Kinnock was given a standing ovation by the meeting which was held in Camera.

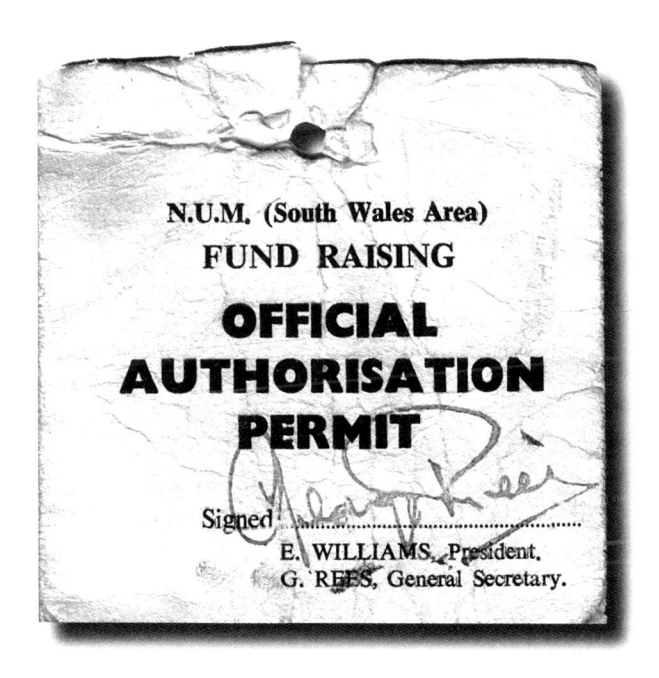

Week 40 - Walker Meets The TUC

At the admission of the Attorney General Sir Michael Havers, the government took an unprecedented step, providing funds to finance the sequestrators in their quest for the NUM's assets. Coming under attack from the Labour benches in the House of Commons, Sir Michael admitted that there was no precedent, but he claimed the move was justified under common law. The Attorney General maintained that the move, which had been requested by the sequestrators, was in the public interest to see that the orders of the High Court were carried out. The view of the opposition was that the government were now seen to be directly participating in the coal dispute by trying to cripple the union's finances. Another consideration, was undoubtedly that having lost a Receiver, they could not allow the courts to lose a sequestrator as well.

Thursday December 13th, the NUM executive met in Sheffield with Mick McGahey presiding in the absence of Arthur Scargill who was defending himself at Rotherham Magistrates Court against the charges of obstruction at Orgreave in May. McGahey reported details of an initiative worked out with the TUC. Seven members of the TUC liaison team would present these to the government. After the meeting Mick McGahey said "We are desperately anxious to end this hardship, but it must be on a principled basis after a valiant ten month struggle. We are anxious to get the NCB back to the negotiating table and I hope it happens immediately" the miners' vice-president also said "Our people are suffering privation it is getting nearer to Christmas and children are involved."

Friday December 14th, the TUC committee had a meeting, lasting ninety minutes, with Peter Walker. The TUC initiative which was put to Mr Walker asked that the NCB should not proceed with its March 6th proposal to close the five pits earmarked for early closure and instead should commit itself to a review of the Plan for Coal. Walker who had been briefed by Ian MacGregor before the talks, was insistent that the NUM must shift its ground before there could be NCB/NUM negotiations, following the meeting Peter Walker said, "There has never been any movement by Mr Scargill from his demand, which is that any pit, no matter how uneconomic, should be kept going until it is exhausted of coal."

Arthur Scargill was found guilty of obstruction by a stipendiary magistrate at Rotherham, he was find £250 with £750 costs. During his trial, Scargill accused the police of 'setting up' his arrest. As he left the court he said, "I anticipated the same kind of anti working class judgement that has been the order of the day during the mining industrial dispute. Even members of the media are beginning to believe it and that is saying something."

Later at a public meeting in Grimethorpe, South Yorkshire he said he had no intention of appealing against the conviction as he had "No faith in getting a fair trial, and certainly no faith in getting a fair judgement from the courts."

The week also saw the death of the former NUM General Secretary Mr Will Paynter aged 81 years. Mr Paynter a former South Wales area president, had been General Secretary at the time of large scale closures of pits in the 1960's, he was an ardent supporter of the current struggle.

Week 41 - The Spectre Of Spencerism

The Nottinghamshire Area Council of the NUM met at their Mansfield headquarters and approved crucial rule changes to the Union rulebook. Mr Justice Warner refused the NUM a High Court order to postpone the meeting. Area President Ray Chadburn denied that the changes heralded the formation of a breakaway union. Attempting to play down the rule change Mr Chadburn said, "The area council has reinforced their decision that this is not a breakaway union, but they are altering the rule to protect them from discipline under rule 51." Rule 51, of course, was the controversial move taken by the special delegate conference in the 18th, week of the strike, which set up a disciplinary procedure.

The Area Council deleted rule 30 from the Nottinghamshire rule book which stated that, "In all matters in which the rules of this union and those of the National Union conflict the rules of the National Union shall apply, and in all cases of doubt or dispute the matter shall be decided by The National Executive Committee of the union." Other rules to give the area greater power were considered, it was, however, decided to defer until January, any move to lift the national overtime ban which was still operational in working areas. Calls for the resignation of the area General Secretary Henry Richardson were ruled out of order.

Nottinghamshire was now in danger of evoking the spectre of Spencerism. Spencerism was the name given to the following of Mr George A Spencer. The national stoppage of 1926 saw defeat when the Nottinghamshire miners returned to work as indeed they had done during the 1st national strike of 1893. Spencer, a right wing Labour MP and miners' leader formed a breakaway company union after the 1926 defeat and with company blessing the collaboration prevailed for a decade or more. Spencer who became General Secretary and his fellow leaders sought to justify the organisation by alleging that the leadership of the Miners' Federation of Great Britain was too 'left.'

Spencer later quit the Labour Party but he remained in Parliament, he died in 1957.

Weeks 42 and 43 - Christmas '84 New Year '85

Christmas was celebrated in the mining communities, many of them now divided, with some men having abandoned the strike tempted by the NCB's Christmas bonus which was made up in the main of monies already owing to the strikers. It is difficult to call a man who has been on strike for nine and a half months a 'scab,' but his brother trade unionists would also have endured severe hardship and yet remained loyally on strike. In many cases the miners who returned to work had been long standing opponents of the strike which puts a question mark against their motive. But motive apart, the actions of these men were undermining their union's ability to secure a negotiated settlement. The NCB were claiming that 31% of the NUM membership were now at work.

The outlook for the NUM was depressing. The condition of many pits, according to the NCB, was desperate. The length of the stoppage meant that the NCBs requirement of production cuts had long been overtaken. The Government were presiding over an economy in shambles, a weak pound and the worst of the winter to come. But while miners were continuing to abandon the strike neither the Government nor the NCB would be anxious to resolve the dispute by negotiated settlement, total victory over the NUM would be far sweeter, never mind the expense which was totalling £5 Billion according to Arthur Scargill, about half that amount according to the official figure being given.

For striking miners and their families some festive cheer was salvaged by the efforts of support groups, the generosity of the public and assistance from other trade unions both in Britain and abroad - a voluntary alternative welfare system had been created.

The work put into Christmas by the women's support groups was a natural extension of the 1st class job they had done throughout the strike to prevent the miners being starved back to work. The minority of strikers in working areas such as Nottinghamshire where an estimated fifteen hundred remained on strike and Leicestershire where only thirty were on strike, faced perhaps the hardest time of all with no natural community support. During the holiday period the strike received a set back with a pledge from Peter Walker, "There will be no power cuts during the whole of 1985 with the coal production that has now been achieved." Mr Walker's statement was clearly designed to sap the moral and resolve of the strikers, as power cuts were potentially the strikers' greatest weapon. For the 1st time in the dispute, the NUM leadership in the form of Peter Heathfield conceded that on present trends there might not be any power cuts. He said, "I accept that if the Government, regardless of costs, is prepared to use substitute fuels in power stations, then with the current level of economic activity, and with a mild winter, it is probable that there will be no cuts the Central Electricity Board will survive on a wing and a prayer." He added, "I never anticipated power cuts once it became clear that the Government was increasing the proportion of oil burnt at power stations from 5% to 47%." Obviously undaunted by this view Arthur Scargill and his wife Anne joined a Christmas Day picket line at Ferrybridge power station in West Yorkshire. Traditionally a time to be both reflective and to contemplate the future, so perhaps this is as good a time as any to take stock of the situation. This will be done by re-examining the leading factors which emerged in 'setting the scene.'

Firstly, if we look at the predicted British Heavy Weight Championship it is quite apparent that Arthur Scargill was winning the intellectual debate with a clear points margin but Ian MacGregor with a better equipped corner was landing the more telling punches. Scargill certainly performed much better than MacGregor in front of the television cameras, the latter appeared shifty and was even unfortunate enough on one occasion to be seen on the news holding a carrier bag in front of his face. But as never before in a major industrial dispute had a union leader to contend with such an onslaught from the establishment united in one common cause. Scargill suffered a bad press throughout geared in the main to his refusal to condemn picket line violence. The press largely neglected to point out that three times as many pickets as police had received medical attention arising out of picket line confrontation. It is also worth noting that in the first week of the strike immediately following the tragic death of the young miner David Jones, the NUM President had called for his members to behave responsibly. The question of refusing a national ballot and of course the Libyan Affair gave the press other sticks with which to beat him. Scargill who since taking over the day to day running of the dispute in the 6th week led from the front ably abetted by his two lieutenants McGahey and Heathfield, whereas, MacGregor resembled a 1st World War General sometimes seeming to have disappeared altogether. Arthur Scargill inspired either fierce loyalty or was regarded as public enemy number one, it was the latter image which was presented daily in the popular press. Even some of the broadsheets were Partisan to the point of sheer farce. At one stage the Sunday Times devoted an article to Scargill's 'blink-rate' which attempted to illustrate the instability of the man caused by pressure. The politics of the 'bogeyman' is a frightening feature of which the vilification of an individual, in this case Scargill, obscures the more important issues being discussed and averts public gaze away from the real focal point.

Secondly we look at the position of Prime Minister Margaret Thatcher and her government whose line was to make pretence of non-involvement in the dispute. To establish the truth one need look no further than the leaked report in the Economist drafted by Nicholas Ridley now the Transport Secretary. Large coal stocks have been supplemented by the import of foreign coal (often mined by children in Columbia, slave labour in South Africa and poorly paid miners in Poland.) Power stations were meeting customer demand without power cuts by greatly increasing the amount of oil being burnt. Non-union labour was crossing picket lines daily in the huge coke and iron ore convoys. But most importantly the way policing had been radically improved, if improved is the right word had, however, brought with it some serious consequences. Incidents of over reaction by police had been one of the major talking points of the strike. Apart from allegations of brutality, some police officers had, allegedly, waved £20 notes at striking miners, that was not policing, that was not an act of neutrality. It was blatant provocation. We had moved one step nearer to a national police force. The National Reporting Centre based at Scotland Yard was opened for business with the strike just two days old, its purpose to co-ordinate the deployment of police from other constabularies into the coalfields. The style of that policing has been paramilitary and there have been allegations that troops were involved. It is fair to say that the dispute has been fought as bitterly in the courts as on any picket line. Successful actions in the High Court had declared the strike unofficial, ruled that the NUM could not enact its own rules, or discipline its own members, and had sequestrated both the National and the South Wales Area assets. These apparent partisan decisions, among others were leading many people, particularly in mining communities to believe that the scales of justice were being weighted. The majority of picket line offences were not for acts of violence, but for minor offences such as obstruction. Some pickets had been charged under antiquated laws such as 'besetting' from the Conspiracy and Protection of Property Act 1875. There had also been instances of changing charges originally brought by police, in some cases additional charges were brought to apply pressure for plea bargaining. The failure of the mass pickets at Orgreave was one of the turning points of the dispute. Unlike Saltley in 1972, the police won the day and raised a question as to the effectiveness of the use of mass picket versus mass police lines. It was the implementation of the 1978 Ridley Report which more than any other factor controlled the direction the strike was taking and laid the lie that the government were not involved.

Finally what of the reluctant dominos – the moderate coalfields? If the strike had been solid it would probably have been settled before Christmas. Would a national ballot have produced a national stoppage? It's a hypothetical question, but it is generally supposed that it would have created unity and made the strike more credible giving the NUM more authority in the prosecution of the dispute, this doubtless seems the case. The absence of the national ballot was used as the main 'get out' clause for moderate leaders of other unions who were able to justify their lack of physical support by pointing to the fact that Scargill had failed to get all of his own members out. The complicated Bersham example is worth considering. At various stages of the strike at the colliery we saw moderate North Wales reject the strike call, But Bersham miners refused to cross a picket line and so joined the strike. They then considered joining forces with South Wales NUM leaving Point of Ayr isolated in the North. In week thirty five, Bersham reaffirmed support for the strike by a slender margin, and then in week thirty seven a return to work accelerated leaving the North Wales area executive to announce the strike had collapsed, Ironically by Christmas there remained more strikers at Point of Ayr than at Bersham. Neil Kinnock began the New Year by appearing on a picket line at the South Celenyn colliery, Newbridge in his Islwyn constituency, where he received a warm welcome from strikers.

Wednesday January 2nd 1985, South Wales police announced that another miner from Rhymney had been arrested and charged with the murder of Mr David Wilkie, he was named as Anthony Williams aged 26, and employed at Markham colliery near Blackwood, Gwent.

Week 44 - The National Executive

The NCB introduced a scheme aimed at breaking the strike in South Wales by arranging organised groups to return to work. If a return could be instigated in that coalfield the national stoppage would almost certainly collapse. There was a flurry of activity from the union to prevent the trickle back turning into a flood. Cynheidre colliery was considered to be the weak link to the coalfield's solidarity. The NCB said that ninety men were now reporting for duty at the pit. Arthur Scargill travelled to Pontberem Miners' Welfare Hall where he addressed six hundred Cynheidre strikers. After the meeting which was held in camera, Scargill said "This dispute will continue until the NCB withdraws its threat to butcher our industry and destroy our communities."

Thursday January 10th, the NUM executive met in Sheffield and approved a plan, previously endorsed by the South Wales area executive and initiated by Welsh Church Leaders. The peace move by the Council of Churches for Wales proposed the setting up of a far reaching independent review body to look at the nation's energy policy as well as considering the nature of the mining communities involved. Backing was also given to a proposition from Northumberland to enlarge the NUM's three man negotiating team to include the full national executive. This move was seen as an attempt to promote a more flexible attitude.

The debate which had dominated the meeting, however, surrounded the rule changes made by the Nottinghamshire Area Council. Notts were given until the 29th of January, when a special delegate conference was due to meet in London, to get back in line.

Friday January 11th, the Nottinghamshire Area Council met at Mansfield and reaffirmed its decision by thirteen votes to one. General Secretary Henry Richardson was the only one present to support the national executive. President Ray Chadburn chaired the meeting, but he did not vote. Richardson was subsequently suspended from office by his Area Council, a decision Chadburn called "diabolical," Peter Heathfield branded the working miners' leaders as the "enemy within" echoing Margaret Thatcher's description of the NUM.

The drift back to work continued, Christmas had been bound to prove a watershed one way or the other. South Wales stayed overwhelmingly solid, but saw the return of twelve men to Six Bells colliery, Abertillery, where there were scuffles between police and pickets, four arrests were made, the trouble allegedly started when a police officer threw a punch at one of the miners as the picket line was dispersing. In West Yorkshire four policemen were injured and four pickets arrested during clashes outside South Elmsall colliery near Wakefield.

The NUR and ASLEF said they would back a twenty four hour strike at eleven key Midland and Yorkshire depots in a week's time. The strike was called to protest against management harassment of railwaymen blacking coal movement.

Week 45 - "General Secretary In Exile"

As Britain experienced its worst weather of the winter and the pound sterling sinking to all time lows against the dollar and some fearing parity, the steady drift back to work continued throughout the coalfields but there was still just over 1% reporting for work in South Wales. Some did, however, return in small numbers at the North Celenyn colliery, Newbridge, at Roseheyworth colliery, Abertillery and at Bedwas colliery near Caerphilly. There were five arrests outside Nantgarw colliery, Blaengarw.

The taxi conveying two rebel working miners to Six Bells colliery was involved in an ambush in the village of Six Bells near Abertillery. Snowballs were thrown at the taxi and a rock said to weigh 8 ½ lbs was hurled through a window allegedly striking the driver, Mr Howard Crothers of Gabalfa Cardiff, between the shoulder blades. The incident happened at a sharp bend in the road less than a mile from the pit at a spot known locally as Brown's Corner. The driver was employed by the Cardiff taxi firm, City Centre Cars. This was the same firm who had employed Mr David Wilkie who had been killed seven weeks previously at Rhymney. A miner from Abertillery, was subsequently charged with the Six Bells offence.

Thursday 17th January, the twenty four hour rail strike went ahead despite a threat from British Rail that they would sue the unions for loss of revenue.

The proceedings at the House of Commons were suspended for some twenty minutes when the sitting was disrupted by a group of Labour MPs led by Tony Benn (Chesterfield.) They were protesting that demands for a debate on the coal dispute were once again refused. When the sitting resumed, in what seemed to be a challenge to the Speaker's authority, Tony Benn said, "A substantial body of members of this house are determined to secure a debate on the miners' dispute in Government time next week." The incident displeased Neil Kinnock who believed that a debate at this time would be damaging to the NUM's cause and he subsequently told a meeting of The Parliamentary Labour Party in no uncertain terms.

The peace proposals by the Council of Churches for Wales were snubbed in a letter from Peter Walker which was dismissive of the formation of an independent review body. It now looked certain that the Government were hoping to see the strike end without a negotiated settlement, but rather, by the accelerating return to work. This view was given more substance when in a radio interview Margaret Thatcher speculating on the defeat of the NUM said, "We shall get real leadership amongst people who believe in real moderate and honest trade unionism. That will be a great achievement."

Henry Richardson became what he himself called "A General Secretary in exile" when Mr Justice Woolf ruled in the high court that Mr Richardson could resume office, but should not carry out the policies of the NUM National Executive from his Mansfield office. This decision added both to the split and confusion in Nottinghamshire.

Week 46 - "Impossible Demands"

Hopes of exploratory talks to lay the foundations for a negotiated settlement flickered throughout the week.

Monday January 21st, the NCB's Industrial Relations Director Mr Ned Smith met Peter Heathfield at a secret location. Smith's deputy, Kevin Hunt was also present. The meeting had apparently been arranged at Mr Smith's suggestion the previous week following a meeting of the Coal Industry Social Welfare Organisation's Joint Council. Progress was made, optimism was in the air and there was confirmation of a basis for further talks, however, disagreement was again the order of the day when the NCB's chief spokesman Michael Eaton said "Nothing following today's meeting brings direct negotiations any nearer." On the other hand Arthur Scargill said "It was agreed that both sides should report back on that meeting to the executive of the union and the board and consider the possibility of a resumption of negotiations." The TUC welcomed the attempted breakthrough, but referring to Mr Eaton's comments, Norman Willis said "We are used to cold water, but we will swim on."

Tuesday January 22nd, hopes were again dashed when Margaret Thatcher told the House of Commons that there was no point in renewed negotiations unless the NUM dropped their "Impossible demands," it may have escaped her notice, but the NUM were in fact not making demands, but resisting the coal board's demands. She brushed aside Neil Kinnock's attempts to stress that the NUM were prepared to enter negotiations "without pre-conditions." The Prime Minister said "Seven rounds of talks have foundered on the essential fact that the leadership of the NUM boast it has not budged an inch."

Wednesday January 23rd, Peter Walker held meetings with Welsh Church leaders and with the Welsh Group of Labour MPs, but neither meeting was fruitful.

Thursday January 24th, Peter Heathfield briefed the NUM executive on his meeting with Ned Smith.

Margaret Thatcher laid down her terms for renewed talks by insisting on a written acceptance of the closure of uneconomic pits from the union. The Prime Minister scented victory and she wanted unconditional surrender. This ugly mood of vindictiveness sparked an angry groundswell of support for the NUM from the Labour and Trade Union movement. Peter McNestry of NACODS was quick to respond to Thatcher's televised demands when he said "If Margaret Thatcher wants to start talking about closing all uneconomic pits, that cuts right across any agreements we have made. If she demands from the NCB that they insist the NUM agree to closure of uneconomic pits, that is something we cannot accept. We have never, ever agreed that with the coal board." Then referring to the Prime Minister's involvement McNestry said "She is out to destroy the NUM. It has become a political strike."

Speaking at a rally in Glasgow Mick McGahey Declared that, "The government is demanding blood, but they are not having the blood of the miners."

Speaking in Gloucester Neil Kinnock condemned Margaret Thatcher's interference and her desire to defeat and humiliate the miners. He said, "I think it would be very foolish if the Conservative Party allowed her to get away with that because it would be an act of self destruction, like Samson pulling in the pillars of the temple."

Amid the uncertainty that existed the NUM wrote a letter to the NCB and it was agreed to hold talks without pre-conditions next week in order to set an agenda for negotiations.

Away from the confusion surrounding the 'talks about talks,' the drift back to work continued in the coalfields. In South Wales the strike was breached for the first time at St John's colliery, Maesteg and at Coed Ely colliery near Llantrisant.

NATIONAL UNION OF MINEWORKERS

**ST. JAMES' HOUSE, VICAR LANE,
SHEFFIELD, SOUTH YORKSHIRE S1 2EX**

President A. SCARGILL
Secretary P. E. HEATHFIELD

Telephone: 0742 700388

Please quote our reference in reply:
Your Ref:
Our Ref: PEH/MF.

1st February 1985.

Mr. M. Spanton,
National Coal Board,
Hobart House,
London, SW1.

Dear Mr. Spanton,

I am in receipt of your letter dated 31st January 1985, and must express great disappointment at the Board's response to the Union's initiatives.

The five proposals of the Union are undoubtedly positive initiatives to provide the basis for resumed negotiations, and pay due regard for what has taken place in the Industry over the past eleven months.

1. PLAN FOR COAL

    This proposal is based upon previous submissions by the Board which have been accepted by the Union.

2. FUTURE OF COLLIERIES/UNITS

    The Union's proposal takes account of the Board's own suggestions when we met with ACAS. This would provide for all matters relating to the future of Collieries/Units to be dealt with in accordance with procedures operating prior to 6th March 1984, and of course the Union have previously accepted an amendment to the procedures to provide for an Independent Review Body, and we feel that the broad recognition given to this proposal during informal discussions could lead to agreement in negotiations.

3. FIVE COLLIERIES

    The Union's proposal accepts that these five pits remain within the procedure on the understanding that undertakings given by the Board within the Procedure will be honoured. This new proposal also provides for any unforeseen major mining problems to be discussed in the normal way, and we feel this point is manifestly fair and sensible.

4. MARCH 6TH PROPOSALS

    The Union's proposal is, of course, a statement of the present situation and has been publicly acknowledged by the Board's spokesman, Mr. Eaton, in an Independent Radio News interview on 31st January.

5. AMNESTY

    It is inconceivable that in any discussions leading to a resolution of this dispute that the question of dealing with those men who have been dismissed in the course of the dispute cannot be a matter for discussion between the National Coal Board and the National Union of Mineworkers.

    Indeed, in my meeting with Mr. Smith on the 21st January, it was acknowledged that the Union would pursue this matter when negotiations resumed.

    It seems a matter of equity that the same principle applied in 1972 and 1974 be applied in the current situation.

I find your refusal to resume negotiations without preconditions extremely disappointing. Should the Board change its mind, however, and decide that it does want to see a settlement of this dispute, I reiterate that the Union's National Executive Committee is available for talks at any time.

Yours sincerely,

Week 47 - An Exchange Of Letters

Tuesday January 29th, the preliminary talks failed to agree an agenda for fresh negotiations after a three hour long meeting between a senior coal-board official, Mr Merrick Spanton and Peter Heathfield. The NUM General Secretary refused the board's request for a written assurance that a negotiated settlement would cover uneconomic pits. The NCB were clearly echoing Margaret Thatcher's sentiments expressed the previous week. Arthur Scargill speaking on Channel 4 news said "The astonishing revelation tonight is that the National Coal Board apparently are beginning to insist upon written assurances about discussions on uneconomic capacity. It has already produced a very strong reaction, I'm told, from NACODS, because it means that the agreement between NACODS and the coal board is absolutely worthless." Scargill added that "The butchery of the industry" amounted to the closure of seventy pits. NACODS' Peter McNestry said later "Everyone has been shouting that the NUM should accept the NACODS agreement. Everyone is now aware that the NUM cannot be offered the NACODS agreement because to give a written agreement beforehand would make their participation in that agreement impossible." The NCB spokesman Michael Eaton said "The central issue is, and it has been made clear, dealing with uneconomic capacity" he also added "I hoped the talks today would form the basis of real grounds for negotiations, but they have not done so. I am disappointed."

Wednesday January 30th, the NUM executive met at Congress House where they were updated on the position. A letter was received by the union from the NCB signed by Merrick Spanton, this added to the confusion. It was addressed to Peter Heathfield and it read as follows:-

I refer to your letter dated 29th January 1985. Your letter states that a number of new initiatives were tabled at our meeting which you believe could produce the basis for a negotiated settlement of the present dispute. At the meeting you said you regarded them as agenda items. I am surprised that you now refer to them as new initiatives. After a short discussion on them yesterday you withdrew the paper and we have no way of recollecting their content. It would be helpful therefore if you would put forward these items again. You will recollect that the main purpose of our meeting was to tell you that the board required the NUM to put forward proposals to provide a basis for the board to determine that it was worthwhile to enter negotiations to reach a settlement of the dispute and that in particular you would address the question of dealing with uneconomic capacity. You said that you would discuss this with your colleagues, and I now await your response.

Thursday January 31st, the board sent the union another letter of similar content demanding an agreement to the closure of uneconomic pits. The NUM executive met with leading Welsh Churchmen. The executive also agreed to stay in London for another day at the request of Norman Willis because of "further developments.

Friday February 1st, the NUM sent the board a detailed reply outlining the union's position to avoid further misrepresentations by the board or government. A copy of the letter sent by Peter Heathfield to Merrick Spanton is included on page 111 to give the full picture. It was becoming increasingly obvious that in pursuit of total victory, both the NCB and government were lifting hopes and then dashing them in order to escalate the return to work. This was a cynical tactic against miners and their families who had suffered extreme privation.

The drift back continued and three policemen were injured during clashes with about three hundred pickets who were trying to prevent men returning at Bedwas colliery in South Wales. There was one arrest outside South Celenyn colliery, Newbridge. In South Yorkshire there were several arrests made amid violent clashes at Houghton Main colliery, near Barnsley. Police used riot gear to disperse an estimated three thousand pickets engaged in a massive show of solidarity at Cortonwood colliery, the main road at Brampton Brierlow was blocked for two hours and the police made five arrests.

In a week when the High Court Receiver Michael Arnold paid the NUM's outstanding £200,000 fine from money he had recovered, it was ironic to read in the Observer newspaper January 27th that the working Nottinghamshire Area NUM had operated a secret fund financed by the NCB since 1947 at the time of nationalisation. The coal board at this time continued a payment which had been made by Notts Coal owners to George Spencer's company union. It was estimated that the annual payment could be as high as £1,000,000.

Week 48 - The Joint Statement

Monday February 4th, began with a record number of men abandoning the strike, the NCB once again dashed hopes of a negotiated settlement by demanding a written undertaking from the NUM stating its willingness to change its position on uneconomic pits.

Thursday February 7th, the NUM executive met in Sheffield, Peter McNestry and NACODS President Ken Sampey were in attendance. After both separate and joint meetings the two unions issued a joint statement:-

"Following a meeting between the joint executives of the NUM and NACODS, it is agreed that there should be immediate negotiations to resolve the long and damaging dispute in the mining industry. To this end, it is agreed that the conditions being demanded of the NUM by the National Coal Board would effectively negate the agreement reached between NACODS and the coal board in October 1984. The fact that the NUM accepted last October the provision under a modified colliery review procedure of an independent review body should in itself provide the basis for a negotiated solution to the current dispute."

The joint proposals were dashed almost immediately when NCB spokesman Michael Eaton said "We have no grounds whatsoever to re-enter negotiations." Prime Minister Margaret Thatcher reinforced this line when she told the Young Conservative conference "If the NUM accept the economic factors must be taken into account in deciding the future of pits, if they accept the right of the board to take the final decision after all the procedures have been completed – then a settlement is ready and waiting."

An idea was being floated in some quarters of the NUM most notably South Wales, for an organised return to work without a settlement. This was seen as a dignified way of bringing the strike to a conclusion and allowing the union to remain intact and therefore live to fight another day. The idea as well as another to call upon the TUC to reconvene Congress was discussed by the NUM executive, but on the strength of the joint statement with NACODS, it was agreed that the strike would continue.

In Scotland the coal board sealed off the main face at the fire ravaged Seafield colliery in Fife and warned that a total of two thousand, three hundred jobs could be lost at both Seafield and the neighbouring Frances colliery, the two pits form a complex, being linked underground.

In South Wales, five pickets were arrested outside Penallta colliery, at Ystrad Mynach, Mid-Glamorgan.

There was a rare success in the courts for the NUM, when at Sheffield Crown Court a jury acquitted eight striking miners who had been charged with the offence of Unlawful Assembly during the pitched battles outside Orgreave coke plant.

Week 49 - Willis Meets MacGregor

A group of working miners in South Wales were granted an injunction by Mr Justice Scott in the high court, to stop picketing at the five pits where they were scabbing. The five pits involved were Cynheidre, Cwm, Abertillery New mine (Roseheyworth,) Merthyr Vale and Abernant. The union said that they could not prevent men turning up at a colliery in order to demonstrate. Mr Justice Scott followed this judgement by outlawing mass picketing at eleven Yorkshire pits. The case was brought by nineteen working miners and his ruling affected the following collieries:

Allerton Bywater, Dinnington, Frickley, Kiveton Park, Maltby, Manton, Manvers Main, Rossington, Shire Oaks, Wath-on–the-Dearne and Yorkshire Main.

Monday February 11th, and the South East regional TUC and the North West TUC both organised a Day of Action to support the miners. There was trouble outside Carrington power station at Sale, Greater Manchester, when an estimated six hundred demonstrators taking part in the North West Day of Action attempted to turn coal supplies away. A police officer had to receive the 'kiss of life' after being crushed between the surging crowd and the radiator grill of a delivery lorry. A senior police spokesman said, "There was an element in the crowd who had nothing to do with mining, including students, who turn up at most of these demonstrations."

Tuesday 12th February, Norman Willis and Ian MacGregor met in a bid to set an agenda for renewed peace talks.

At Oakdale colliery near Blackwood the NCB expressed concern that the pit could flood, pit bottom pumps had been submerged by thousands of gallons of water. The Coal board had angered the local NUM lodge after appealing for miners to return to work to save the pit. The appeals were made by loudspeaker vans touring the area. The withdrawal of safety cover by the union was in protest at the return to work of four miners.

Wednesday 13th February, the South Wales area NUM held a delegate conference and decided to call for a national delegate conference to "discuss all aspects of the strike."

Four NACODS leaders met Peter Walker and Coal Minister David Hunt in an attempt to achieve a resumption of NCB/NUM talks.

The week ended with the now customary confusion surrounding the peace negotiations. The NUM Executive was standing by, expressing willingness to re-enter talks without preconditions. Both the NUM and NACODS were at Congress House endeavouring to prepare a draft agenda and ACAS announced its readiness to assist.

Week 50 - Negotiations by Proxy

Sunday 17th February, the TUC called for an urgent meeting with the Prime Minister after failing to set up fresh negotiations. Six hours of talks between Norman Willis and the NCB deputy chairman Mr James Cowan had proved fruitless. During the talks between Messrs Willis and Cowan the NCB chief confirmed that the board's commitment to the NACODS agreement was absolute. Norman Willis had presented an amended version of the NACODS agreement to the NCB on behalf of the NUM, Arthur Scargill said that the proposals "Should have resulted in a resumption of negotiations immediately to deal with other such aspects of the dispute such as the Coal board plans announced on the 6th March 1984, the future of the five collieries and an amnesty for those who have been dismissed during the current dispute."

Tuesday 19th February, the seven man TUC delegation met the Prime Minister at Downing Street. Margaret Thatcher was joined at the hour long meeting by Lord Whitelaw, leader of the Lords, Tom King and Peter Walker. The Prime Minister was said to be firm but polite to the TUC team, but it was clear that Thatcher scented victory and was relying on the continued return to work ending the strike. Margaret Thatcher asked Peter Walker to convey to the NCB the TUC view that the board and the union were not far apart. After the meeting the TUC team returned to Congress House and although they returned empty handed the fact that the meeting had taken place at all seemed quite remarkable however, it would be a mistake to read too much into the apparent softening of the Government's tone.

Wednesday 20th February, the NUM Executive met at Congress House and after a three hour meeting unanimously rejected an initiative aimed at achieving a peace formula. The document under discussion by the Executive had been sent to Arthur Scargill by Ian MacGregor and was acknowledged by the TUC as the best which could be achieved in the prevailing circumstances. The unanimous rejection by the union was made in the belief that if anything had changed it was a hardening of the NCB's attitude. The NUM's basic disagreements were a withdrawal of the March 6th 1984 proposals on the reduction by 4,000,000 tonnes a year and withdrawal of closure of the five ear-marked pits. The NUM insisted that any trial document should make no reference to the NCBs right to determine closure of pits on economic grounds. Apparently, both the TUC and the NCB believed that their negotiations had overtaken these sticking points. The reduction in capacity had been rendered irrelevant by the length of the strike and that the five pits would be considered under the NACODS agreement. When the meeting ended the Executive were unanimous in their opposition to the contents of the document and roundly condemned proxy negotiations via the TUC, Scargill said, "We are not prepared to sign away the jobs of our members." Lancashire Leader Sid Vincent said, "We are in a worse position than we were on Sunday. We have got nowhere at all. We are being conned. They are trying to make fools of us." Cumberland's Leader Harry Hanlon said, "It's ended in tears. We've been taken for a ride." Trevor Bell of COSA said, "We are disgusted by what we've been told. The strike will go on in the coalfields. It's up to the lads now."

Thursday 21st February, Congress House was a venue for the NUM's, delegates conference, and conference unanimously approved the continuation of the strike. An acrimonious atmosphere had developed between the NUM and the TUC and as he left the conference Peter Heathfield said, "It's an incredible situation to try to negotiate by proxy." Arthur Scargill said, "I think the TUC has seen at first hand the duplicity of the NCB. I only hope the TUC will now go out in a public way campaigning for the decisions of the TUC Congress and call on the trade union movement to support the miners." Referring to the document Henry Richardson said, "Chamberlain came back with a better paper in 1939." The most scathing personal criticism of Norman Willis came from Dennis Murphy the Northumberland President who said, "The TUC has been messenger boys in a situation which they do not understand. I would not say we have been misled at all, but if you send a boy on a man's errand, you are bound to have problems." It is clear from the unanimity of opinion that a genuine misunderstanding existed between the NUM and the TUC, and that the TUC had misinterpreted its role during the exploratory talks with the NCB. In the House of Commons Peter Walker stated that, "There is no way that Mr Scargill's absurd and extreme demands are going to be met." The Energy Secretary said the NUM Leaders had, "Slapped the TUC in the face." Later Dennis Skinner (Labour Bolsover) was ordered to leave the Commons and was suspended for the rest of the day, after John Biffen deputising at Question Time for the Prime Minister who was in Washington, had falsely accused Mr Skinner of arguing for months for a TUC/Government meeting. Mr Skinner angrily retorted "That's a lie," and "Not me, I never asked that question-check the record Mister." The Speaker intervened and asked the MP to withdraw his un-parliamentary language, refusing to do so Dennis Skinner said, "He told the lie, not me." Such is the nature of our quaint way of doing the nations business.

Meanwhile, back in the coalfields, some miners' leaders were afraid, that the continued failure to achieve a negotiated settlement would turn the return to work into a flood. In South Wales the leadership had become increasingly concerned although the area was still the bedrock of the strike, the area NCB were offering a £325 holiday bonus to miners returning to work.

At a meeting attended by approximately four hundred people, Mr Terry Thomas the South Wales area NUM Vice President continued the attack on the TUC when he called on ordinary rank and file trade unionists to take action over the heads of their leaders and he called Mr Willis "An errand boy." The meeting at Abertillery Leisure Centre was also addressed by Tony Benn, Michael Foot, Llew Smith MEP and Dr Kim Howells.

By the end of the week the TUC agreed that its Finance and General Purposes Committee should meet the NUM to review the position.

When Miners Organise

They Face Repression

IMPRISONED, physically assaulted, robbed of their basic civil rights, miners and their families are fighting for their lives.

Thatcher has decided to smash the N.U.M. by dismantling the coal industry, regardless of the cost and consequences to the country.

Since the strike began, over £1 billion has already been wasted on this criminal nonsense. N.C.B. chairman MacGregor has received millions to add to his private fortune. Tinpot generals in every police headquarters in the land have been awarded fat salary increases to encourage their officers to act like animals on the picket lines.

The Social Security laws have been manipulated to starve miners' families back to work. At magistrates' courts miners are facing fines and bail conditions more suited to a South American dictatorship than an English county.

Forty years ago on the beaches of Normandy our soldiers died protecting us from the Nazis and their police state. Now Thatcher is encouraging her little Hitlers in Scotland Yard to crawl from under their stones and destroy what freedoms remain.

SUPPORT THE MINERS
DEFEND YOUR FREEDOM

Week 51 - An Organised Return To Work?

Sunday 24th February, on the second occasion during the strike, violence flared on the streets of London. A march and demonstration organised by the South East region of the TUC in support of the miners attracted a large crowd estimated at fifty thousand by the organisers, although the police put the figure at fifteen thousand. The trouble began when most of the demonstrators had already arrived at their Trafalgar Square destination after a march at Hyde Park. The initial scuffles broke out between demonstrators and police near Horse Guards Parade. There were several arrests and the marchers then refused to move on until those arrested had been released. Mounted police were deployed; missiles were thrown at the mounted officers. Women and children caught up in the crush had to be lifted over railings to comparative safety. Five police were hurt as were five demonstrators and there were one hundred and twenty one arrests. A police spokesman blamed "drunken hooligans," but the organisers and march stewards blamed police behaviour which was described as unnecessary.

Monday 25th February, saw a record return to work in the coalfields. Men, who had remained loyal from day one, were giving in as a result of severe hardship and the feeling of hopelessness being created by the NCB building up hopes only to dash them again. The pattern of the big return continued throughout the week. In South Wales, Tower colliery at Hirwaun the head of the Cynon Valley, was breached by a solitary working miner for the first time.

Wednesday 27th February, the NCB were claiming that more than 50% of NUM members had now abandoned the strike. The strike now almost twelve months old looked in danger of crumbling. Although, this would not necessarily be a quick process as the pattern of the return had tended to level out from time to time. Even if 50% were now back at work, by the coal boards own figures 29% of NUM members had not answered the strike call in the first place, this makes the 50% figure seam less impressive. The resolve of the hard core of strikers remained steadfast.

The TUC were working overtime trying to salvage a deal for the NUM, and, not least, to show their conduct in the dispute, in a better light. So with the strike obviously in its final stages, a national delegate's conference was called for Sunday March 3rd. An organised return to work without a signed agreement was the way out in the opinion of some areas, The South Wales leadership were in the vanguard of this movement. Other traditionally militant coalfields to follow this line were Scotland and Durham, Lancashire, Northumberland, North Derbyshire, The Durham Mechanics and COSA were all, also, committed to this option, arguing defeat would be avoided and the dispute brought to a disciplined and dignified closure. Yorkshire and Kent favoured a continuation of the strike until an amnesty for miners sacked during the dispute had been achieved. The latter option was favoured by the National leadership.

THE FIGHT GOES ON!

NO VICTIMISATION!

RELEASE IMPRISONED MINERS!

NO PIT CLOSURES!

Miners Support Cttee Hackney

Week 52 - The Strike Ends And The Immediate Aftermath.

Sunday 3rd March, at Congress House, the National Executive met immediately before the special delegates' conference. South Wales called for an organised return to work without an agreement. The Executive split 11-11 with Arthur Scargill casting his vote for the status quo. When the delegates were asked to endorse the status quo they voted to return to work, this was moved by Terry Thomas the South Wales Vice-President, and carried only just by 98 votes to 91. Scargill emerged to announce the decision to a crowd made up in the main by a large contingent of Kent miners demonstrating outside Congress House. Scargill said, "Conference decided that the NUM should organise a return to work on Tuesday, and that the dispute in the industry will continue until its aims are completely fulfilled and in particular there is an amnesty for those dismissed in the dispute." There was a furious reaction from the demonstrators, but Arthur Scargill said, "I can only come out here and reflect the decision of the conference, which was taken democratically."

Tuesday 5th March 1985, this historic day saw the organised return to work, miners marching back with both pride and defiance. Much media attention was forecast on the return of the men at Maerdy colliery in the Rhondda Valley. The village of Maerdy had long been dubbed Little Moscow in grudging tribute to its proud and militant tradition. The Maerdy NUM lodge had stayed solid to a man for the duration of the dispute, so it became the focal point of the dignified return. The miners, joined by their supporters, marched back to the pit beneath banners and behind the Maerdy, Ferndale and Tylorstown Colliery brass band. The national return, however, was not without its setbacks, about thirty thousand miners refused to return until demands for an amnesty for over nine hundred miners sacked during the strike. Kent's three pits stayed almost solid whilst there were only partial returns in Scotland and Yorkshire. Kent sent pickets into other coalfields in a vain attempt to keep the strike going. At Barrow colliery near Barnsley the return was led by Arthur Scargill. The march was halted by pickets at the colliery gates. Arthur Scargill promptly led the men away again.

As the week wore on amid acrimony and confusion, Scotland voted to return to work and was later followed by Kent.

The NCB announced the loss of fifty jobs and thirty transfers from South Celenyn colliery Newbridge. Incidents between strikers and scabs were widespread as could be expected after such a protracted and bitter struggle. Small localised disputes flared and the NCB were in belligerent mood, saying that miners must work with each other, and must lift the overtime ban before pay talks could take place. They stated that there would be no amnesty for men who had been dismissed for violence or vandalising NCB property. The strike was over, the aftermath of this unparalleled post war struggle and its consequences were only in their infancy.

'There are some defeats more triumphant than victories.'
Michel de Montaigne, French essayist (1533 - 1592.)

Aftermath - The Legacy Of Bitterness

The strike left an immeasurable mark on all parties concerned. It also left more questions than answers. Both the National Union of Mineworkers and its members had been crippled financially, the union to the tune of a staggering £24 million. The cost to the miners and their families was huge. Personal debt was the factor which eventually led to the overtime ban being lifted after seventeen months on April 2nd1985, thus clearing the way for pay talks which led to a 5.2% settlement. In July at the NUM annual conference, further rule changes precipitated Notts into forming a breakaway union, the so called Union of Democratic Mineworkers under the leadership of Roy Lynk and David Prendergast, both of whom had been sacked as NUM officials by conference delegates for their conduct during the dispute. They had led the working miners in Nottinghamshire. They were charged by conference with encouraging area rule changes which had brought Nottinghamshire into conflict with the national union. Consequently they were in breach of contract by supporting the dismissal of Henry Richardson as the Area General Secretary. Mr Lynk had replaced Mr Richardson as General Secretary – the spectre of Spencerism had indeed risen.

Had the NCB made a tactical error in allowing the dispute to end without a signed agreement? More importantly had the dispute in the absence of a negotiated settlement even ended? The dispute was in danger of developing into industrial guerrilla warfare given the obvious tensions which existed in pits up and down the British coalfields, pardon the pun, the dispute was in danger of going underground. Even Ned Smith recently retired as the NCB Industrial Relations Director questioned the board's wisdom in failing to achieve a negotiated conclusion.

By the time of the NUM conference in the first week of July the NCB had already announced the closure or merger of twenty five collieries, many without even bothering to consult NACODS. It was apparent that the NACODS agreement was not worth the paper it was written on and that the NCB was in ruthless mood in pursuit of their spoils of war. NACODS leadership had lost a lot of credibility and had put their rank and file in a difficult position. Arthur Scargill speaking at the conference called the return to work "A fundamental mistake."

Should the TUC have done more? It seems inconceivable that the General

Secretary in his meeting with the Prime Minister had failed to warn that with ten wage claims from other unions on the table government intransigence would lead to the opening up of a second front. Surely it would be incumbent upon any TUC General Secretary to make the government aware of hazardous consequences.

Leaders of the Labour movement seem able to relate to the achievements of the past, to walk proudly beneath the banners of days gone by, to commemorate the Tolpuddle Martyrs and the Chartists who fought to change bad laws. They are romantic about Labour history, but when history is in the making that is a different story altogether. During a tour of the Far East, Margaret Thatcher boasted at Kuala Lumpur that the miners' strike had been "seen off." She complimented the realism of other unions who had not come to the miners' support. Her comments triggered an indignant response at home. Gerald Kaufmann called her "The enemy abroad." But, indignation apart, the Prime Minister's remarks touched a sore point, when she praises the lack of support there can be no greater indictment than that.

What Of The Political Parties? Unexpectedly Labour made a recovery in the opinion polls immediately following the end of the strike. In many ways the strike had highlighted that the strength of this Prime Minister could easily become her weakness. One also suspected the Labour recovery vindicated the political judgement of Neil Kinnock. Although, sometimes he had seemed mesmerised by the opinion polls, he'd had to walk a tightrope representing a mining constituency with four pits and presenting himself as an alternative Prime Minister. He never gave the unequivocal support to the NUM - which Margaret Thatcher afforded the NCB. The Nottinghamshire affair looked set to cause future problems. The UDM stated it would seek both TUC and Labour Party affiliation. Five marginal parliamentary constituencies in Nottinghamshire would need to be won if Labour are to form the next government. Kinnock would not want to choose between alienating the electors in Nottinghamshire or the NUM and a large proportion of left wing support in the rest of the country. The Alliance leaders, particularly Dr David Owen had adopted an anti-Scargill stance which at times emulated the government.

In the coalfields, in the mining communities the bitterness and the recriminations continued. Rebels were singled out, disciplinary action by the NCB against intimidation in turn led to localised disputes flaring up. One of the worst reported incidents involved a leading back to work campaigner Mrs Joy Watson, a brick was hurled through her car window after taking her husband, Paul to work at the Phurnacite plant at Abercwmboi, South Wales. The violence, however, was not one-sided. Mick McGahey was the victim of an unexplained and brutal attack by two men outside his Edinburgh home. No prosecution was ever brought.

A cloud of gloom again descended on the South Wales valleys, when two miners were found guilty of the murder of taxi driver Mr David Wilkie. The coalfield was shocked by the severity of the life sentences imposed on Dean Hancock and Russell Shankland. The third miner Anthony Williams was acquitted, but was still sacked by the coal board's summary justice. There was no amnesty for sacked men as in 1972 and 1974, reinstatement was considered individually and was completely arbitrary.

Perhaps it would be as well to end with another question central to the strike itself. What future for the mining communities now?

One thing is for certain things would never be quite the same again.

What I have discussed above was written in the weeks that followed the end of the Great Coal Strike of 1984-85. Even with the benefit of a quarter of a century of hindsight, I find it difficult to see things in too different a light, however, I am sure most people will agree that the "Titanic Struggle" ended in defeat for the National Union of Mineworkers something I would not willingly admit twenty five years ago. Although, perhaps the then Bishop of Durham David Edward Jenkins, was right when he warned of defeat for the miners, the government and the country. For those that would claim victory it was indeed a pyrrhic victory. By their own admission the strike cost the government £6 billion, this was presumably a conservative estimate! The closing paragraphs of this book will look again at the main protagonists of the momentous event and inquire Where are they now :-

MARGARET HILDA THATCHER, Baroness Thatcher of Kesteven (born October 13th 1925) continued as Prime Minister until 1990 having won three General Elections. She also continued looking for enemies and found them at home, in Northern Ireland, in Europe and in the Persian Gulf. Her government's introduction of the Community Charge (The Poll Tax) in 1989 led to riots, most seriously in Trafalgar Square in March 1990 where there were some two hundred thousand protesters, began her rapid political decline. Her stance on European policy led to her Deputy Prime Minister Sir Geoffrey Howe resigning. His resignation speech on November 13th 1990 was the catalyst to Michael Heseltine's leadership challenge and her fall from power, just nine days later she was succeeded by John Major. Speaking at Ystradgynlais in 1992 Michael Foot said "The greatest political leaders must combine courage and imagination. If you've only got courage, you may just turn into stubbornness, and for us, that's the nicest thing you could say about Mrs Thatcher I suppose." (Jones 1994 p544) Now elderly, frail and forgetful she is still a 'spectre at the feast' of both Conservative and Labour Parties.

ARTHUR SCARGILL (born January 11th 1938) continued as President of the NUM until 2002 and is still Honorary President. At the start of the strike in March 1984 there were one hundred and seventy collieries nationwide, by the time Scargill left office there were fifteen still working. The number of closures proved Arthur Scargill right over and over again. In fact it far exceeded his dire predictions.

Scargill's conduct during the strike has long since divided opinion. Should the NUM have held a national ballot? The strike was called in accordance with the union's rules and was official within the rule book no matter what the judiciary declared. Did mass picketing work? Arthur Scargill believes there should have been more, used strategically, to target power stations, ports, cement works, steelworks and coking plants. Reflecting in the Guardian (March 7th 2009) he wrote "Orgreave coking plant was a crucial target for mass picketing. I knew that its coal supplies could be cut off as had been the case at the Saltley coke depot in Birmingham in 1972; a turning point after which that particular strike was soon settled." Another bone of contention was picket line violence, however, it is worth considering "Most of the picket lines were peaceful, but the mass pickets Scargill organised at key pits ran into violent clashes with the police. Some police were injured, but so were many miners, thirty nine of them while picketing Orgreave. They later won £500,000 in damages and costs from the South Yorkshire Police for the injuries inflicted on them." (Castle 1993 pp 569/570.) Denis Healey a long standing contemporary of Barbara Castle wrote, "Scargill made every tactical and strategic error in the book. He called the strike when coal stocks were high and the demand for coal was at its lowest. Then when the strike was only a few months old, he turned down a compromise which even the Communist Vice-President of the union regarded as a victory." (Healey,1989 p 504.) It has, however, always seemed to me that Arthur Scargill was not responsible for the timing of the strike. It was called in response to a NCB announcement to close five pits.

Arthur Scargill left the Labour Party when it abandoned Clause IV of its constitution in 1995 giving up its commitment to nationalisation enshrined in the beautifully drafted words of Sidney Webb in 1917, "To secure for the workers by hand or by brain the full fruits of their industry and the most equitable distribution thereof that may be possible upon the basis of the common ownership of the means of production, distribution and exchange and the best obtainable system of popular administration and control of each industry and service." Scargill founded the Socialist Labour Party in 1996 which has become yet another bit player on the extreme left wing of British politics.

In May 2002 the Editor of the Daily Mirror, Roy Greenslade made a profound apology to Arthur Scargill and Peter Heathfield after the French Supreme Court ruled that former NUM Chief Executive Roger Windsor repay a debt of £29,500. This goes someway to vindicating a wronged man. The series of stories printed by the press and emanating from Robert Maxwell's Daily Mirror in 1990, accusing Scargill of paying off his mortgage following the strike with monies donated by Libya, resulted in Greenslade's offering his sincere apology in the Guardian May 27th 2002 "I know sadly some old friends and colleagues won't appreciate this mea culpa. But lingering embarrassment is far outweighed by my heartfelt delight in being able, at last, to put the record straight by saying sorry."

SIR IAN KINLOCK MACGREGOR (born September 21st 1912 died April 13th 1998) retired from the NCB in 1986. His closure programme prepared the industry for privatisation in 1994. His anti trade union activities saw him rewarded with a knighthood in 1986. MacGregor died of a heart attack at Taunton, Somerset in 1998.

NEIL GORDON KINNOCK, Baron Kinnock of Bedwellty (born March 28th 1942) continued as Leader of the Opposition and of the Labour Party until 1992, when he resigned following defeat at the General Election, his 2nd defeat as party leader. From 1995-2004 he served as a European Union Commissioner, in January 2005 the former left wing firebrand took his seat in the House of Lords.

The miners' strike was a baptism of fire for a young Leader of the Opposition. As with Scargill opinion is divided over the contribution he made during the strike. "Neil's behaviour during the strike had been perfectly correct, but like me he had little use for a general whose egoism had led his troops into an avoidable defeat and opened the way for the further conquests that a triumphant Margaret Thatcher was now planning" (Castle 1993 p 570.) Whereas Scargill argued, "If Thatcher had lost the Tories would have dumped her as they did in 1990. Kinnock didn't see what Wilson did and even Foot did in 1981. If he had supported the strike openly and called on other workers to support it I believe Thatcher would have fallen and Kinnock would have become Prime Minister." (Gardiner 2009.)

Bibliography

Castle B	Fighting All The Way, Macmillan 1993
Cornwell J	Collieries of Western Gwent, Brown and Sons 1983.
Crick M	Scargill & The Miners, Penguin 1985.
Gardiner B	We agreed deal with Thatcher Government, Guardian, 07/03/09.
Goodman G	The Miners' Strike, Pluto 1985.
Healey D	The Time of My Life, Penguin 1990.
Horner A and Hutt GA	Communism and Coal, Dorrit 1928.
Jones Mark	The Story of David Gareth Jones. New Park Publishers 1985.
Jones Mervyn	Michael Foot, Victor Gollancz 1994.
Labour Research Dept	The Miners' Case, 1984.
Miller Jill	You Can't Kill the Spirit, Womens' Press 1986.
Miller Joan	Aberfan A Disaster and its Aftermath Constable 1974.
Page Arnot R	South Wales Miners (Glowr de Cymru). Cymric Federation Press 1975.
Powell D	The Power Game, Duckworth 1993.
Richards F	The Miners' Next Step, Junius.
Routledge P	Scargill, Harper Collins 1993.
Scargill A	'We could surrender or stand and fight' Guardian 07/03/09.
WCCLP	Striking Back, 1985.

Acknowledgements

Newspapers:	The Guardian, The Times, Western Mail, South Wales Argus, Manchester Evening News, Nottingham Evening Post, The Observer, Sunday Times.
Journals:	Coal News, The Miner, The Record, Labour Weekly, Tribune.
Other:	Abertillery Womens' Support Group, Abertillery Museum.
Photographs:	Steve Thomas, Barbara Hetherington, Special thanks to Tony Shott for allowing Steve to photograph Tower Colliery.

Also: Mrs M Parfitt, Mrs K Ross, Mrs L Robins, Sue Roberts, D Cooper, M Challenger, M Tucker, Llanhilleth Open Mic, C Smith, Llanhilleth Institute, St Iltydds Communities First, D Bearcroft, Abertillery Museum, G Bartlett, R Welch, Alan Thomas, Anna Chard, Sue White, Ken Sullivan.

Miner's Badge: Available from - www.nelson-trafalgar-badges.co.uk

Steve Thomas
Design And Print
01495 726220
stevetomas58@freenetname.co.uk